IRO

SOVIET RUSSIA

BY

MICHAEL NEWTON

Iron Curtain Killers

"Serial Murder in Soviet Russia"

By
Michael Newton

"This is a work of nonfiction. No names have been changed, no characters invented, no events fabricated."

RJ Parker Publishing

ISBN 13: 978-1987902433

ISBN 10: 1987902432

www.RJPARKERPUBLISHING.COM

Published in United States of America

Copyrights

Acknowledgments

Thank you to my editor, proofreaders, and cover artist for your support:

~ Mike ~

Aeternum Designs (book cover), Bettye McKee (editor), Lorrie Suzanne Phillippe, Marlene Fabregas, Robyn MacEachern, Kathi Garcia, Vicky Matson-Carruth, Linda H. Bergeron, Sandra Miller

Table of Contents

Introduction

The Union of Soviet Socialist Republics — Soviet Russia, or the USSR — was spawned by apocalyptic violence: an estimated 9,347,000 casualties in World War I (1914-17), followed by revolution, assassination of the ruling royal family (1918), territorial war with Poland (1919-21), and a civil war (1917-22) at home with 3.9 million more casualties, aggravated by intervention from various foreign governments including that of the United States.

Officially established as a one-party Marxist-Leninist state in December 1922, shunned and denied diplomatic recognition by much of the Western world, the USSR labored for decades under the thumbs of ruthless dictators blamed for sweeping genocide, while battling through a Second World War (1939-45) with at least 40 million more citizens slain or wounded.

In the postwar era, Soviet leaders spared no effort — or human lives — in their bid to modernize industry and agriculture, at the same time annexing the bulk of Eastern Europe, imposing strict censorship and elaborate domestic spying, persecuting racial and religious minorities. By March 1946, British Prime Minister Winston Churchill declared that "an 'Iron Curtain' has descended across the continent" of Europe, impenetrable save by Western spies.

Once established in power, leaders of the USSR described their sphere of influence as a "Socialist paradise" on Earth, claiming that as such, it was entirely free of "decadent Western crimes" such as racketeering and serial murder — which itself would not possess a formal name until 1961.

Sadly, they were wrong. Dead wrong.

In fact, the Soviet Union had yet to be born on paper when its first known serial killer surfaced. He was Vasili Ivanovich Komaroff, dubbed "The Wolf of Moscow," a horse trader who, with wife Sophia, killed at least 33 victims between 1921 and 1923. The couple's efficient *modus operandi* involved luring male customers to their stable where Vasili plied them with vodka, then slit their throats or bludgeoned them with hammers, robbing their corpses, afterward placing their bodies in trash bags for burial or dumping them into the Moscow River.

In 1921, while civil war preoccupied authorities, Vasili snuffed out at least 17 lives in that fashion. Sophia first learned of his crimes in 1922, taking the news calmly and pitching in to help her husband. Moscow police soon linked the slayings of 21 men, whose bodies were dumped around the Soviet capital on Thursdays and Saturdays. At first, they overlooked Vasili Komaroff, believing him to be a normal family man, though neighbors were aware of his penchant for domestic violence — once trying to kill his own eight-year-old son. By early 1923, investigators knew that Vasili patronized a local horse market regularly but never brought animals to sell on Wednesdays or Fridays, the days before corpses were dumped. On those days, he chatted with would-be buyers and usually took one home with him — the last time any of those men were seen alive.

In early 1923, police turned up at Komaroff's home, asking questions about bootleg liquor. He evaded them by leaping from a window and fleeing on foot, leaving his latest victim under a haystack, but they captured him on March 18 in Moscow Oblast (region). By that time, Sophia had confirmed her own role in the string of slayings. From his cell, Vasili confessed to murdering 33 men, describing murder as "an awfully easy job" and leading police to bodies they had not yet recovered. Only 29 were found in all, with four dead unaccounted for, but it would be enough. The court convicted Vasili and imposed a death sentence, meting out the same penalty for Sophia. While awaiting execution, Komaroff botched three suicide attempts, but his firing squad had better luck on June 18, 1923, executing Vasili and his wife with a barrage of rifle fire.

Thus came modern serial murder to Russia's "Socialist paradise," and it continues unabated to the present day, unhindered by glasnost and perestroika in 1985-87, or by the final collapse of Soviet communism in 1991. *Iron Curtain Killers* presents 26 cases of Russian serial killing, recorded from the 1960s into the 21st century. Police may no longer deny that such crimes occur in Russia, but as we shall see, they still fall short of solving serial cases, even in the present day.

1. Vladimir Ionesyan: "The MosGaz Killer"

In retrospect, Soviet journalists would say that Vladimir Ionesyan (called Volodya in some reports) was born to "a rather intelligent family" from Tbilisi, Georgia, in 1937. Renowned in childhood as a talented singer, Ionesyan was encouraged by his parents to develop his musical gift — at least, that is, before his father drew a seven-year prison term for commercial fraud. Almost overnight, Vladimir's life veered off course, leading to his arrest for theft at age 17, resulting in a five-year sentence. The trial judge suspended that term, but Ionesyan seemingly learned nothing from his brush with incarceration. By 1959, at age 22, he was back in prison, serving two years for evading the Soviet Union's mandatory military service.

Paroled from that sentence, Ionesyan married and fathered a child, acceding to his young wife's wishes that they leave Georgia and settle in Orenburg, 918 miles southeast of Moscow in Orenburg Oblast, on the boundary of Europe and Asia and close to the USSR's border with Kazakhstan. There, he joined a musical comedy theater, acting and singing for a living. Family life soon paled, however, when Ionesyan met and fell in love with ballerina Alevtina Dmitrieva. In short order, Vladimir deserted his wife and child, moving with Alevtina to Moscow, where they hoped to start a new life.

Unfortunately for their dreams of connubial bliss, Ionesyan could not shake the lessons learned from hardened convicts during his sentence for draft dodging. Rather than seek honest work as a singer or at some other trade, Vladimir devised a scheme to burglarize apartments, where and when he could gain easy access. Vladimir's ploy was to pose as a worker for MosGaz, the sole supplier of natural gas to Moscow's residents, whose employees carried out routine inspections and made repairs citywide. He lacked proper credentials, but the plan required none. If he knocked and found no one at home, he could break in and loot the flat. Conversely, if a man answered, Vladimir could make some excuse and move on. If a woman or child was at home — well, that was their hard luck.

Ionesyan claimed his first known victim in December 1963, when he stabbed a 12-year-old boy multiple times, then fled with 60 rubles in cash ($1.04 in America), a sweater, a bottle of cologne, and a pair of sunglasses that caught his fancy. Shifting to Ivanovo, 158 miles from Moscow, he killed twice more, adolescent girls aged 14 and 16, knifed to death in separate attacks. In the latter case, Vladimir took time to rape the victim before killing her and mutilating her body. Back in Moscow once more, he fatally stabbed an 11-year-old boy in one apartment, then used an axe to slay his final victim, a 46-year-old woman, before stealing a television from her flat.

As luck would have it, a policeman on his beat saw Ionesyan leaving with the TV set, loading it into his truck. Because the Moscow force did not share information on serial crimes — much less alert the public to impending danger — the officer jotted down two digits from Ionesyan's license tag, then forgot about them until the latest victim was discovered in her apartment.

More by luck than any deft police work, Soviet Militsiya detectives focused on Ionesyan as a person of interest, but they were unable to find him. Alevtina Dmitrieva proved more accessible, and she soon cracked under questioning, admitting Vladimir's role in the ongoing crimes. Arrested on January 12, 1964, Ionesyan stood trial on five counts of murder and was convicted across the board, executed by a firing squad with minimal delay, on February 2. For receiving stolen goods, such as they were, Dmitrieva drew a prison term of 15 years.

In death, however, the third-rate musical comedy actor found a kind of immortality. Around Moscow and farther afield, pranksters took to knocking on the doors of friends or total strangers, whispering, "MosGaz calling" to provoke fearful reactions. Parents who'd been left in ignorance of Ionesyan's crimes while he was still alive now used him as a kind of homegrown bogeyman, warning troublesome children that "MosGaz will get you" if they did not mend their ways.

Nor was Vladimir Ionesyan forgotten in the 21st century, achieving a kind of stardom he had never gained in life. During 2012, Andrey Malyukov directed a short-lived television series titled *MosGaz,* in which the names of real-life characters were changed, while poetic license dramatized the cruel apartment creeper's crimes.

2. Boris Gusakov: "The Student Hunter"

Boris Vasylevych Gusakov was born in 1938 to alcoholic parents in the Saltykovka district of Balashikha, Moscow Oblast, located on the Pekhorka River one kilometer east of Moscow Ring Road. Given his family situation, he displayed symptoms of mental illness at an early age, but the onset of World War II left the Ministry of Health's Federal Biomedical Agency little time to care for individual children in crisis. Despite his problems, Gusakov graduated from a state-owned secondary school — the Soviet equivalent of high school — but pursued no higher education and sought work as a photographer instead.

Too young to fight and die in the "Great Patriotic War" against Germany and Japan, Gusakov joined the Soviet Army in 1958, as required by law, and served in uniform until 1961. Married shortly prior to his enlistment, he sired his only child a decade later, in 1968, but by that time his life had taken an irreversible turn for the worse.

Soon after his military discharge, in 1961, a court convicted Gusakov of theft. No record survives of any time spent in prison, but by May of 1962 he was employed at a film-processing factory called Kartolitografii, where employees found him affable enough until he moved on to another job in August 1965. That new position found him printing photographs and films for the Soviet Ministry of the Interior, a vast department that included not only Moscow's city police, but also the dreaded *Komitet gosudarstvennoy bezopasnosti* — the Committee for

State Security or KGB. From there, in January 1967, Gusakov moved on to work as a photographic engineer at an oncology and chemical research facility, but he was dismissed from that position in January 1968 for "violating labor discipline." A series of odd jobs ensued to make ends meet, then May of 1968 found him back with the Ministry of the Interior, laboring in the Moscow Police Department's darkroom.

Unknown to Gusakov's employers and coworkers, by that time he had become an active sexual predator, raping his first young female victim in December 1963. Several more assaults followed over the next six months, before he killed his first rape victim — an 11-year-old schoolgirl — on June 21, 1964. Perhaps shaken by his first murder, Gusakov waited eleven weeks before striking again, when he raped and murdered a young woman on September 4.

Another, longer hiatus in slaughter ensued, and Moscow police officially closed his first two murder cases in early 1968. On March 11 of that year — two months before assuming his position with the police department — he attacked, raped and murdered two female students at the Moscow Power Engineering Institute, a prestigious institution founded in 1930, whose graduates included Li Ping, fourth premier of the People's Republic of China (1987-88), and Ion Iliescu, future two-time president of Romania (1989-96 and 2000-04). Happily for Gusakov, the institute's large student body gave Moscow police no end of suspects to consider, including both native Russians and foreign students from friendly communist nations. Detectives overlooked their man entirely, never guessing that the killer might be squirreled away in their very own darkroom, developing crime scene photos.

In April 1968, Gusakov struck twice more. First, he waylaid and raped a nine-year-old girl but neglected to kill her. Later that month, he attacked a strolling couple, beating the man unconscious, then raping and slaying his female companion. Perhaps Boris believed he'd also killed the male victim, but he was wrong. The man survived to describe his attacker for police, although it did not lead to an immediate arrest.

On May 16, 1968, Gusakov approached two naïve tenth-grade girls in Serpukhov, Moscow Oblast, and persuaded them to join him for a picnic in the country. Arriving at their destination, he first tried to poison the teenagers, but failed at that and whipped out a meat cleaver, chasing them through the countryside. This time, luck turned against him, as the fleeing girls encountered a policeman, who in turn arrested Gusakov.

Legal maneuvers delayed Gusakov's trial until 1969, when Moscow's criminal court convicted him on five counts of murder, plus various lesser felonies. Newspapers labeled Gusakov "The Student Hunter," since most of the females he'd slain or attempted to kill were enrolled at various schools. Sentenced to die, Gusakov filed several pleas for clemency, but all were rejected. In 1970 he met his fate before a Moscow military firing squad.

3. Anatoly Slivko: "The Collector"

Anatoly Yemelianovich Slivko blamed an accident for his descent into child molestation and serial murder, but psychiatrists believe the seeds of evil had been planted long before he turned his hand to sadism and slaughter. The truth, in either case, went with him to his lonely grave.

Slivko was born on December 28, 1938, at Izerbash, located on the coast of the Caspian Sea in the Dagestan Autonomous Soviet Socialist Republic. That "Land of Mountains" — now the Republic of Dagestan — is situated in southern Russia's North Caucasus region. Its capital and largest city, Makhachkala, stands 35 miles northwest of Slivko's birthplace. As an adult, Slivko moved to Stavropol, the capital of Stavropol Krai (district), also in the North Caucasus region.

There, he met future wife Lyudmila, a coworker with the Vladimir Lenin All-Union Pioneer Organization, or Young Pioneers, Russia's equivalent of the Boy Scouts. They embarked upon a curious sort of courtship, during which they never kissed or touched, but which still led to marriage—especially difficult for Anatoly, an insomniac with a poor appetite, repulsed by his own appearance and reluctant to engage in sex with Lyudmila. When they conceived two children during 17 years together, Lyudmila regarded it as something of a minor miracle.

Outwardly, meanwhile, Slivko pursued what seemed to be a normal life — at least, that is, until age 22, in 1961. The turning point came when he witnessed a fatal traffic accident. A motorcyclist lost control of his bike and swerved into a crowd of pedestrians, killing an adolescent boy dressed in the uniform of a Young Pioneer. As Slivko told police, decades later, "The boy had experienced convulsions in his death throes as the smell of gasoline and fire permeated the air. I felt the attraction to boys for the first time in my life. There was a lot of blood and gasoline on the asphalt, the smell of gasoline and fire. I suddenly felt a desire to hurt a young boy like him. The feeling haunted me, and I had to move far way to make the desire disappear. But after five or six months, after an ejaculation during sleep, the same excitement rose again and consistently pursued me."

Even so, Slivko waited two more years before acting on his perverse desire. By then, he had moved his family to Nevinnomyssk, Stavropol Krai, straddling the Bolshoy Zelenchuk River, 34 miles south of Stavropol. There, he bought a youth club to attract potential prey, catering specifically to members of the Young Pioneers.

Like most other serial killers, Slivko preferred a certain type of victim, normally aged between 13 and 17 years, or small for his age if older. Beginning in 1963, Slivko ingratiated himself with boys who fit his pattern, winning their confidence before he introduced them to a special "experiment" of his own device. It involved "controlled hanging to unconsciousness," designed to stretch the youth's spine and render him insensate, while Slivko filmed the procedure and vowed to revive the boy promptly, unharmed. A key requirement was the uniform. If his selected target was not a Young Pioneer, Slivko himself would buy the outfit and provide a pair of freshly polished shoes.

The "game" had rules, of course. To prevent vomiting, Slivko warned his volunteers to avoid food for several hours beforehand. Then, once the youth was dangling unconscious before him, Slivko would strip him naked, fondle him, and film his prostrate form in suggestive poses before masturbating over the body. Afterward, dressed once more and warned to keep silent, the boys were unaware of what had happened to them after they passed out.

Between 1963 and 1985, he later told police, Slivko persuaded a total of 43 boys to try his "experiment." He revived 36 of those as promised, while murdering the other seven, dismembering their bodies and torching them with gasoline, to further replicate the original traffic fatality. He filmed each stage of the grisly procedure, and retained the murdered victims' shoes as trophies of his kills.

Slivko murdered his first victim, a 15-year-old runaway named Nikolai Dobryshev, on June 2, 1964. He later claimed the death was accidental, occurring when Slivko could not revive the teenager after hanging him. As a precaution, he also destroyed the film and still photos he'd snapped of the "experiment" gone wrong.

If true, the accidental death did not dissuade Slivko from seeking new victims. His second murder — and, allegedly, the first he planned — claimed the life of one Aleksei Kovalenko in May 1965. A few months later, fire swept through his first youth club, but Slivko acquired another in 1965, calling it Chergid. His "experiments" continued, Slivko filming both his molestations and group outings of Young Pioneers, but another seven years elapsed before he killed again. That time, 15-year-old Aleksander Nesmeyanov disappeared from Nevinnomyssk on November 14, 1973, presumed by the police to be a runaway.

Flash forward another 18 months, to May 11, 1975, and Slivko's next confessed slaying. Victim Andrei Pogasyan was 11 years old and a Chergid club member — as was Aleksander Nesmeyanov before him. His mother refused to believe that her son had vanished voluntarily, telling police instead that he had gone off to a local forest, where "a man" filmed gatherings of Young Pioneers. Authorities already knew Slivko, but they dismissed him as a suspect, noting that his films had been honored with several awards.

During the winter of 1975, a prison inmate claimed to know where Aleksander Nesmeyanov was buried, but police found nothing at the site and filed his testimony away as a hoax. In 1980, another Chergid member, 13-year-old Sergei Fatsiev, disappeared, followed in 1982 by 15-year-old Vyacheslav Khovistik. Again, police had no corpses, no evidence. Their verdict: still more runaways. Slivko's final victim was 13-year-old Sergei Pavlov, missing after telling a neighbor he was off to meet the owner of Chergid.

Pavlov's disappearance piqued the interest of prosecutor Tamara Languyeva, who opened an investigation of his case. She found no evidence of criminal activity at Chergid, but interrogation of the club's young members revealed several who described Slivko's "experiments" and spoke of suffering "temporary amnesia" afterward. Even then, it was December 28, 1985, before police arrested Slivko at home, charging him with seven counts of murder, seven counts of sexual abuse, and seven counts of necrophilia.

In custody, Slivko was a compliant prisoner. During January and February 1986, he led police to the graves of six dismembered victims, but could not locate the seventh, first victim Nikolai Dobryshev. Trial proceeded in June 1986, resulting in Slivko's conviction on all counts, as confessed. Sentenced to death, he spent three years on death row in Novocherkassk, Rostov Oblast, while police seized the opportunity to pick his twisted brain.

In 1989, detectives were particularly eager to discuss an ongoing series of murders around Rostov, with 29 victims and counting to date. Slivko provided what insight he could, but brought them no closer to murderer Andrei Chikatilo (see Chapter 9), who would remain at large and active until November 1990. Finally, on September 16, 1989 — hours after his last police interview — Slivko was called from his cell and led to a supposed shower room, where an executioner dispatched him with a single pistol shot into his brain.

4. Anatoly Utkin: "The Ulyanovsky Maniac"

Anatoly Viktorovich Utkin drew his first breath in Ulyanovsk, the administrative center of Ulyanovsk Oblast on the northern edge of Russia's Central Steppes, in 1943. His father missed the birth, preoccupied like millions of other Russians by waging war against the invasive forces of Adolf Hitler's Third Reich. By the time he returned from combat, his son Anatoly was a toddler, already learning to appreciate Ulyanovsk Oblast's deciduous forests, steppes and meadows, separated by Europe's longest river, the Volga.

As a teenager, Anatoly attended a vocational school, part of dictator Josef Stalin's massive effort to modernize Soviet industry and agriculture. He emerged to follow in his father's footsteps with the Red Army, driving heavy trucks and UAZ-469 utility vehicles, the Soviet equivalent of Western jeeps.

Murder would have to wait.

Utkin claimed his first victim, a nine-year-old girl, at Barysh, the administrative center of Baryshsky District in Ulyanovsk Oblast, at age 25, on March 31, 1968. After raping and strangling the girl, he stole her wristwatch, then drove her corpse 190 miles away from the crime scene, where it was discovered two months later.

After the first killing, Utkin picked up his pace. On June 27, 1968, he raped and murdered a 17-year-old girl, then repeated the attack on September 25 with a 13-year-old in Penza Oblast, bordering Ulyanovsk Oblast to the west. He botched his fourth attack, on

October 8, when the girl fought him off and escaped with her life. On November 28, he raped and killed a 10-year-old girl in Ulyanovsk, inexplicably stealing her left stocking before he fled. Six months later, on May 28, 1969, he murdered an adult woman in Ulyanovsk.

Soon after that attack, police intervened—but they only charged Utkin with robbery, still clueless as to his involvement in a string of local slayings. Convicted on that relatively minor charge, Utkin received a three-year prison term and was paroled in October 1972.

True to form for a serial killer, Utkin struck again soon after his release from custody, but once again his luck turned sour. His intended victim, an adult woman this time, resisted forcefully and managed to escape. On December 6, 1972, Utkin claimed his only male victim, bludgeoning a man, stealing his cash, and dumping his body in a roadside ditch. In retrospect, that victim was probably a hitchhiker, like the woman Utkin killed nine days later. Victim and slayer met by chance at Ulyanovsk Baratayevka Airport, and the woman gratefully accepted Utkin's offer of a ride into Ulyanovsk, 5½ miles northwest of the airport. She never made it, being raped, murdered and robbed before Utkin discarded her like trash along the way.

Criminals often come to grief when they abandon a familiar *modus operandi*, and Anatoly Utkin was no exception. On February 8, 1973, he tried to rob a textile factory in Ulyanovsk, killing a cashier in the process, then found he could not open the company safe containing workers' payrolls. Frustrated, he set the factory on fire with a bucket of diesel fuel, brought along for that very purpose, then forgot to take away the metal bucket with his name stamped on it. Police found that clue when the ashes cooled, and Inspector Anwar Melnikov nabbed Utkin at home on February 9. His efforts to resist proved fruitless, and he soon wound up in jail.

Confronted with one murder charge, plus arson and attempted robbery, Utkin decided to confess his other crimes. At trial, in 1974, Judge Vitaly Shorin convicted Utkin on nine counts of murder, plus robbery and theft, imposing a sentence of death. Legal appeals delayed his execution until September 12, 1975, when it was carried out by a military firing squad.

5. Anatoly Biryukov: "The Hunter of Babies"

Every normal parent's worst nightmare involves losing a child. Disease and random accidents may strike at any time, but homicide is doubly cruel, depriving parents of their progeny simply to sate a killer's lust for blood. During the 1970s, one such malignant predator was active in the Soviet Union, bringing heartache to five innocent families.

The monster whom reporters dubbed "The Hunter of Babies," Anatoly Nikolaevich Biryukov, was born in Moscow on February 18, 1939, celebrating his second birthday 18 weeks before Adolf Hitler's "Operation Barbarossa" sent Nazi troops flooding across the Soviet Union's western borders. By October 1941 Moscow was besieged, the site of a four-month battle that produced an estimated 1.4 million casualties on both sides, leaving much of the capital city in ruins. Anatoly's father, Nikolai Biryukov, was in the thick of it, emerging with a general's rank and a gold star marking him as a Hero of the Soviet Union, wartime Russia's highest decoration for service to the Soviet state and society.

Decades later, some critics would say that Nikolai Biryukov's heroism helped to mask his son's atrocious crimes or, at the very least, prompted homicide investigators to soft-pedal them for fear of embarrassing Anatoly's father.

As an adult, after finishing his mandatory service in the Red Army, Anatoly Biryukov married and fathered several children. Normal fatherhood and family life, however, did not quell the dark urges he had begun to feel inside. At age 38, on September 16, 1977, he finally surrendered to that twisted drive, kidnapping an infant when its mother left the child unattended in a stroller on Marshal Biryuzov Street in Moscow, outside an infant formula store. Searchers found the pram that afternoon, empty, abandoned. Soon afterward they also found the missing baby stabbed to death in the hallway of a nearby apartment house.

Clearly, the kidnapping and murder had been crimes of opportunity — but who would stoop to such an act?

Biryukov struck again on September 19, stealing a second child and stroller parked in front of the Children's World store on Moscow's Prospekt Mira. That time, the search took longer. It would be October 17 before police found the missing infant's body, sexually assaulted and stabbed, dumped at a landfill near Mamyrov, a village on Moscow's outskirts.

No genius was required to link the vicious crimes, but Soviet officialdom still stubbornly denied the existence of serial killers stalking the USSR. In that atmosphere, Biryukov felt free to choose another victim, attempting his third public kidnapping in Chekhov, the administrative center of Chekhovsky District, south of Moscow. Overconfidence nearly doomed him, prompting pursuit by a group of neighbors, and while he escaped to murder his victim, those who'd chased him furnished homicide detectives with a clear description of their man. Even then, however, Biryukov eluded capture long enough for the police to blame him for two additional infant murders, committed before his arrest.

Conviction at trial, in 1978, was a foregone conclusion. Sentenced to death, Biryukov attempted suicide in prison but was foiled and placed under close observation, to prevent him from frustrating justice. Next, he filed an appeal before the Supreme Soviet of the Russian Soviet Federative Socialist Republic, but that body swiftly rejected his plea for clemency. On February 24, 1979, six days after Biryukov's fortieth birthday, a firing squad ended his wasted life.

Still, memories of Anatoly Biryukov linger in modern Russia. In the 21st century, Moscow's NTV television network featured Biryukov's case on its series dealing with historic crimes, *The Investigation Led...* An episode titled "The Empty Stroller" reviewed his crimes, including taped interviews with one young victim's mother, two state investigators, two eyewitnesses from Chekhov, and Biryukov's former defense attorney. Leonid Kanevsky, the show's presenter, first floated the notion that Soviet authorities avoided publicizing Biryukov's crimes, at least in part, because of his father's status as a decorated hero from World War II.

6. Aleksey Sukletin: "The Alligator"

Cannibalism, practiced around the world for centuries as a religious ritual or to avert starvation during famines, is today regarded as the ultimate taboo in civilized society — except, that is, among the relatively tiny population of serial killers. A surprising number of those predators — roughly three out of 100 among those captured — indulge at some point in eating human flesh. And Russia's slayers are no exception.

Another child of World War II, Aleksey Vasilevich Sukletin was born in 1943, in Kazan, the capital and largest city of Tatarstan, ranked as the eighth most populous Russian city. Sprawling over 26,000 square miles at the eastern edge of European Russia, Tatarstan claims the motto *Bez Buldırabız!* ("We can!"), a fair statement of its natives' determination to survive disasters such as the epic famine of 1921-22, during which half of its population expired. While Nazis never reached their territory during World War II, more than 560,000 Tatars joined in that struggle, with more than 300,000 of them killed.

Aleksey Sukletin passed largely unnoticed till age 36, living with girlfriend Madina Shakirova in Vasilyevo, a small town near Kazan, where he worked as a watchman at a gardening supply store. Secretly, however, he harbored a bad case of vorarephilia, characterized by the erotic desire to consume another person. Finally, in November 1979, he could wait no longer and laid plans to act on those feelings, with full cooperation from his live-in lover.

The couple's first victim was 22-year-old Ekaterina Osetrova. Sukletin used Madina Shakirova as bait, distracting Osetrova with conversation while he crept up behind her, stunned the woman with a hammer blow, then cut her throat. That night, and in the days to come, Aleksey and Madina devoured most of their victim's body, finally disposing of the rest where they were certain it would not be found.

As prosecutors later explained that first crime: "He informed Shakirova about his intention to systematically commit the murders of females for subsequent consumption and demanded that she help him in these murders. After receiving Shakirova's consent, Sukletin led Osetrova into a room and entered into sexual relations with her, after which Shakirova, offering a drink, began to distract the victim, and Sukletin struck her with a hammer wound in rag. Then he put Osetrova in a trough brought by Shakirova and cut her throat with a knife. After the murder, with the help of Shakirova, Sukletin dismembered her. Part of the corpse they buried in the ground, and used some for food."

And with that experiment behind them, they only wanted more.

Their killing pace accelerated rapidly in early 1980, with Sukletin murdering Tatiana Illarionov on January 13 and dismembering the corpse with Madina's help, while Madina kept the victim's passport. February's prey was 15-year-old Rezeda Galimov, whose sweater Madrina kept for herself, followed by Nadezhda Sityavina in March and Natalia Shkolnikova in May. July of 1980 evoked Madina Shakirova's first objection to the ongoing murders, when Sukletin raped and murdered 11-year-old

Valentina Elikova, whom he'd lured home with an offer of pay to clean his house. Madina did not mind the crime so much, but instead balked at the victim's tender age, sparking an argument that ended their relationship. Madina moved out and returned to the home of her parents.

Unwilling to continue on his killing course alone, Sukletin soon found another lover, 23-year-old Lidiya Fyodorova, and adopted one of her relatives, Anatoly Nikitin, as a bar-hopping compatriot. When Sukletin broached the subject of murder and cannibalism, however, Lidiya refused to go along. Instead, Sukletin changed his *modus operandi,* selling human flesh to neighbors with the explanation that he'd purchased more beef or pork than he could use.

When Lidiya discovered Aleksey's new hobby, she threatened to expose him. Troubled by the risk, Sukletin recruited Anatoly Nikitin to neutralize the threat. Together, on March 12, 1985, they murdered Lidiya, first subjecting her to 14 hours of rape and torture before Sukletin cut her throat. Afterward, the two men sat down to a cannibal feast, afterward hiding the remainder of Lidiya's corpse in a transformer box and burning her clothes with diesel fuel.

But time was running out for The Alligator and his sidekick. First, Madina Shakirova returned to live with him again, hearing the first-hand story of Lidiya's death, then cleaning up Sukletin's house and even laundering Lidiya's bloodstained underwear. Whether she broke thereafter and summoned police remains unknown, but officers arrested Sukletin in summer 1985 for killing Lidiya Fyodorova, and he saw no further reason to stay silent, naming Madina and Anatoly Nikitin as willing accomplices to his crimes.

While searching Sukletin's home, police recovered evidence including a bucket half filled with melted human fat. Excavation of his garden soon revealed four bags filled with human bones.

An insanity plea is the common defense to such crimes, but forensic psychiatrists deemed Sukletin to be sane within Russia's legal definition of that term. Two years after his arrest, in 1987, the Supreme Court of Tatarstan convicted Sukletin on seven counts of murder, plus consuming human flesh, imposing a capital sentence. A firing squad performed his execution that same year, on July 29.

For their parts in the cannibal spree, Madina Shakirova and Anatoly Nikitin each received 15-year prison terms. Authorities paroled Madrina in 2002 and she returned to her hometown in Vasilyevo. At press time for this book, no further information was available on Anatoly Nikitin's fate, with online research stymied by his relatively common name — including, among others, a musician who served as principal cellist of St. Petersburg's philharmonic orchestra for over 40 years.

7. Sergei Ryakhovsky: "The Hippopotamus"

Russians have an apparent fondness for nicknaming serial killers after wild animals. They dubbed Aleksey Sukletin "The Alligator" for his consumption of human flesh. Eight years later, they would call Sergei Ryakhovsky "The Hippopotamus" based on his hulking size, although before his capture he was labeled "The Balashikha Ripper" after his birthplace in Moscow Oblast, less than a mile east of Moscow Ring Road.

At first glance, Balashikha seems an unlikely hometown for a serial slayer. Situated on the Pekhorka River and known for its unique system of waterways, its name translates as "Land of Celebrations" or "Land of Laughter and Fun." During the Soviet era, Balashikha became a major industrial center with factories involved in metallurgy, aviation, cryogenic technology, and production of machinery. Many of its sons were sacrificed in World War II, opposing the Nazi invasion.

Sergei Vasilyevich Ryakhovsky was born on December 29, 1963, in Balashikha's Saltykovka district, long known for attracting artistic folk whose numbers included author Leo Tolstoy and landscape painter Isaac Ilyich Levitan. A late bloomer, by age 20 Ryakhovsky had grown to six feet six inches tall, tipping the scales at 280 pounds. That same year, he began to feel "an irresistible desire for intimacy with a woman," but rather than simply dating, he made several attempts to rape elderly women in Golyanovo, one of the largest districts in eastern Moscow.

Captured after one of those attacks, Ryakhovsky was convicted on a charge of "hooliganism" and sentenced to four years in prison.

Whatever befell him in custody, Sergei emerged with a new obsession: a personal mission to "cleanse" Russian society by killing homosexuals and prostitutes. He struck first in 1988, murdering a gay man in Bitsa, a village on the outskirts of Moscow. Before year's end, he killed three more homosexuals in Izmaylovsky Park, one of the largest parks in Moscow and a favored trysting spot for lovers of all sexual inclinations after nightfall.

Despite that energetic launch to his crusade, however, Ryakhovsky proved himself erratic in his choice of victims during his five years of murder for pleasure. Most of those he killed were aged women, echoing his would-be rape victims from Golyanovo, but he also killed five men and two teenagers. Sergei's methods also varied to include stabbing and strangulation, either with his bare hands or a rope. Most victims suffered postmortem mutilation, chiefly to their genitals, and some of their corpses were ravished in fits of necrophilia. In January 1993, Ryakhovsky killed a 78-year-old man, decapitated him with a hunting knife, then returned to his crime scene the following day, severing one of the dead victim's legs. With his next-to-last victim, a 16-year-old boy, Ryakhovsky first hanged the youth, then disemboweled and decapitated him.

Variation in a killer's *modus operandi* always makes work harder for detectives, prompting them to think of multiple slayers at work. Such was the case with Sergei Ryakhovsky, and like other random slayers, his downfall would come about almost by accident.

Specifically, police were scouring one crime scene when they found a decrepit, unoccupied shack with a hangman's noose dangling from one of its rafters. Surmising that an unknown subject might have left the noose as preparation for another murder, they stood watch over the place until April 13, 1993, when Ryakhovsky walked into their trap and they pounced, arresting him without a struggle. Although carrying a knife when he was captured, Ryakhovsky later admitted that the ambush surprised him and froze him with fear.

In custody, Sergei was an accommodating prisoner. He freely confessed to 19 murders, leading officers to various crime scenes and describing the attacks in detail. Despite suggestions of a personal crusade, he claimed that most of his crimes were unplanned, resulting from chance encounters and a sudden, irresistible impulse to kill. Such was the case with a 70-year-old woman and a 78-year-old man he met on separate occasions, while hiking woodland trails. The sole exceptions, he maintained, were the three homosexuals he killed at Izmaylovsky Park in 1988. Most of his victims were in their forties or fifties, with three over 60, while the youngest was 14 years old.

Psychiatrists from Moscow's Serbsky State Scientific Center for Social and Forensic Psychiatry examined Ryakhovsky prior to trial, reporting that his necrophiliac impulses stemmed from a malfunction in his central nervous system, but that diagnosis would not save him. All found him legally sane, a judgment that infuriated Ryakhovsky to the point where he ceased all cooperation with police, recanted his jailhouse confessions, and called for "punishment" of the doctors who examined him. In the midst of Russia's 1993 constitutional crisis between President Boris Yeltsin and the Supreme Soviet (parliament), Ryakhovsky supported the latter, writing a letter to Acting President Alexander Rutskoy that claimed he — Ryakhovsky — was a blameless victim of the "anti-national authority."

All of Sergei's efforts proved futile, however. Convicted of multiple murders at trial, in July 1995, he received a sentence of death by firing squad. Defiantly, he rose in court and told the judge who sentenced him, "I will be back."

And so he was, after a fashion. In 1996, pending Russia's admission to the Council of Europe — unrelated to the European Union but sometimes confused with it in print — Russia imposed a moratorium on future executions. Ryakhovsky was one of many beneficiaries, his death sentence commuted to a term of life imprisonment at a maximum-security penal colony in Solikamsk, a salt mining center in Perm Oblast. Future killers might still face death, however, under Article 20 of the Russian Constitution, which reads that "until its abolition, the death penalty may only be passed for the most serious crimes against human life," and then only at jury trials. Said crimes meriting potential execution include murder with specific aggravating circumstances, "encroachment on the life" of law enforcement officers, and genocide. If executions are performed, they should be carried out "non-publicly by means of shooting."

If Sergei Ryakhovsky thought his life sentence would someday make him eligible for parole, he was mistaken. Perhaps unknown to him, he suffered from tuberculosis, long untreated, and it claimed his life in prison on January 21, 2005.

8. Valeriy Asratyan: "The Director"

Motives for serial murder are as diverse as the killers themselves. Some are driven by an impulse to slay strangers at random. Others stalk victims based on some pattern that attracts them: race, age, choice of clothing or cars, even an address or occupation. And for others, murder is a simple matter of expediency, carried out to silence witnesses who might report some other crime.

Valeriy Asratyan (spelled "Hasratyan" in some reports) was born in 1958 at Yerevan, the capital and largest city in the Armenian Soviet Socialist Republic, as well as one of Earth's oldest continuously inhabited settlements. Yerevan is situated on the Hrazdan River, near Mount Arafat, the site where Islamic prophet Muhammad delivered his farewell sermon to Muslims in 632 A.D. Muslims also say that it is the place where Adam and Eve landed on Earth after falling from Heaven. Yerevan has been Armenia's capital since 1918, two years before Russian troops invaded from the northeast and made the country part of the Soviet Union.

All that was ancient history to Asratyan during his childhood in a stable family deemed prosperous by Soviet standards of the time. No evidence exists of child abuse suffered when he was young, another break from the typical background of serial killers. His parents thought little of his penchant for "playing doctor" in kindergarten, persuading female classmates to disrobe and let him "examine" various parts of their bodies. At age 13, likely unknown to other members of his family, Asratyan enjoyed his first act of sexual intercourse with a 28-year-old woman, and from that day forward, he could never get enough.

In secondary school, Asratyan voiced an interest in psychology. After graduating in 1975, he enrolled at Khachatur Abovian Armenian State Pedagogical University in Yervan, a state university named after a 19th-century author who vanished mysteriously in 1848. Since its foundation in 1922, the university has specialized in training teachers and other educational staff, producing notable alumni that includes playwright Zhirayr Ananyan, actor and producer Davit Gharibyan, film director Hovhannes Galstyan, and Movses Gorgisyan, a leading advocate of Armenian independence. For his part, Valeriy Asratyan pursued a degree in "preschool psychology and pedagogy (teaching)," though his real interest lay elsewhere.

Soon after entering the university, Asratyan read *Lolita*, the controversial 1955 novel by Russian-American author Vladimir Nabokov, in which a middle-aged literature professor becomes sexually involved with his 12-year-old stepdaughter. The novel reflected Asratyan's obsession with young girls and prefigured the crimes that would eventually seal his fate.

Graduating from the university in 1980, Asratyan first worked as a psychologist at a school for children suffering from polio and cerebral palsy. A year later, he married a Muscovite woman and moved with her to Russia's capital, shortly thereafter embarking on rapes of young girls. Police soon captured him, and he was sentenced to a penal colony for two years, emerging in 1984. Almost immediately,

Asratyan resumed his predatory ways and was arrested yet again in 1985, drawing another two-year sentence that put him back on the street in 1987.

Paroled a second time, Asratyan briefly moved to Valuyki, a town in Belgorod Oblast, located at the confluence of the Valuy and Oskol Rivers, nine miles north of Russia's border with Ukraine, but he soon tired of his new surroundings and returned to Moscow. There, his wife was less than pleased to see him, barring Asratyan from her home and filing for divorce. Unfazed, he met and wooed another woman with a 14-year-old daughter, entering a civil marriage and enjoying sex with each before somehow persuading both mother and child to become his accomplices in serial rape.

Asratyan's *modus operandi* involved prowling the neighborhood around Moscow's Children's World Department Store, near Lubyanka Square and KGB headquarters. Carrying fake identification to win his victims' trust as a psychologist, he dosed girls with powerful psychotropic drugs, including antipsychotics and tranquilizers, waiting for them to pass out before he raped them, also stealing whatever cash or other valuables they carried. The drugs, as Asratyan planned, left his victims addled, stricken with amnesia and unable to provide authorities with reliable accounts of the attacks.

In February 1988, Asratyan abandoned his psychologist persona and reinvented himself as a film director, inviting young victims to his apartment for "auditions" for roles in nonexistent movies. In a typical case, he dosed the victim's coffee with psychotropic drugs, raped her for several hours, then dropped her off at a railway station in the Podolsky District of Moscow

Oblast, south of the capital. Police found the girl, but she typically remembered nothing, much like dozens of others, some held drugged at Asratyan's apartment for days on end.

And soon, he began to kill as well.

Asratyan claimed his first murder was accidental, resulting from an unintended overdose of date-rape drugs, but he was clearly not put off by homicide. After leaving that victim on a bench at a railway station, he stabbed a second girl fatally, and drowned a third in his bathtub. He did not kill consistently, however, and in 1990 he allowed one girl to live whose memory was not wholly obliterated by the drugs she had consumed. In fact, she not only described Asratyan and the neighborhood where he lived, but also told authorities of his approach to snaring victims as a film director. Armed with that information, Moscow police staked out female officers in plainclothes, and Asratyan invited one of them home for a "casting," whereupon she arrested him.

In jail, Asratyan confessed to three murders and an uncertain number of rapes. His estimate was "more than 10," while police placed the final tally at 20 victims or more. Having seen the way convicts treat child molesters in prison, Asratyan demanded execution at trial, and the court obliged him after reviewing his record. In 1991, a prison guard dispatched him with a single shot to the head.

Asratyan's story does not end there, however. Years later, journalists learned that he had impregnated one of his surviving victims, who eventually told her parents that she was expecting. They conveyed her to an abortion clinic, but doctors there were barred from operating by the advanced development of her fetus.

She carried the child to term, and while her identity went unpublished, sensational stories speculated on the continuation of The Director's bloodline and what might become of his son or daughter.

9. Andrei Chikatilo: "The Rostov Ripper"

Officially, Andrei Romanovich Chikatilo is Russia's most prolific serial killer, though police suspect others of beating his dubious record. After his arrest, he confessed to slaying 56 victims during his 12 active years as a predator, but a shortage of evidence sent him to trial for only 53 murders, with one case resulting in acquittal. Nonetheless, it was an awesome total, more than justifying his several nicknames as "The Red Ripper," "The Rostov Ripper," and "The Butcher of Rostov."

Chikatilo was born on October 16, 1936, in the village of Yabluchne in Ukraine's Sumy Oblast, 75 miles from the district's capital at Sumy and 208 miles from Kiev, the capital of Ukraine. His parents were collective farm workers — the equivalent of American sharecroppers — who occupied a one-room shanty and worked without pay aside from the right to cultivate a small personal garden. Decades later, Chikatilo claimed he never tasted bread until age 12, often joining his family for meals of grass and leaves to ward off starvation. His mother also told him that one of his brothers, four-year-old Stepan, had been kidnapped and eaten by neighbors during Ukraine's epic famine of 1932-33, caused by Josef Stalin's ruthless effort to expand and modernize Soviet agriculture. Today, that man-made famine is dubbed *Holodomor* ("to kill by starvation"), with estimates of its final death toll ranging from 2.4 to 12 million persons.

When Germany invaded Russia in June 1941, Chikatilo's father was drafted into the Red Army, later wounded in battle and captured. Over the next three years, Andrei witnessed the horrors of Nazi occupation, including aerial bombings, artillery barrages, and mass executions by Adolf Hitler's *einsatzgruppen*, murder squads that hunted Jews, Slavs, and other "undesirables." In all, an estimated 7 million Ukrainians died by war's end in 1945. After Nazis burned the humble Chikatilo home, Andrei was reduced to sharing a bed with his mother—and receiving frequent beatings when she found he was a chronic bed wetter. During the same period, his mother gave birth to a daughter, Tatyana, probably the result of rape by a German soldier.

Despite those trials, Chikatilo still began his formal education in September 1944, though hunger kept him weak and scrawny, a target for bullies who mocked his fainting spells. Myopia gave him headaches and restricted his ability to read in class, yet he somehow became an excellent student, the only one from his collective farm to graduate in 1954.

Puberty's belated onset only added to Andrei's problems, bringing chronic impotence to amplify a stifling shyness around females. In 1953, trying to "cure" himself, he attacked an 11-year-old friend of his younger sister, ejaculating for the first time as she grappled with him on the ground.

After graduating in 1954, Chikatilo applied for entry to Moscow's Lomonosov University — now Moscow State University — established in 1755. He passed the entrance examination with good-to-excellent scores but was still rejected, administrators citing poor grades from his secondary school, while

Chikatilo blamed his father's "tainted" war record of capture by the Nazis. Rather than applying to another university, he traveled to Kursk, the administrative center of Russia's Kursk Oblast, and worked as a laborer for three months before enrolling at a vocational school to become a communications technician.

That same year, 1955, Chikatilo entered upon his first serious romantic relationship, with a 17-year-old girl. They attempted intercourse three times, but Chikatilo still suffered from erectile dysfunction and the girl broke up with him 18 months later.

Graduating from his vocational school, Chikatilo then moved to Nizhny Tagil, Sverdlovsk Oblast, in the Urals, while he took correspondence courses in engineering from the Moscow Technical University of Communications until the Soviet Army drafted him in 1957. He served in uniform until 1960, first as a border guard in Central Asia, then with a KGB communications unit in Berlin, and joined the Communist Party in 1960, shortly before his discharge.

Back in civilian life, Andrei returned to his parents' home in Yabluchne and began dating a divorcée, but he ended that relationship after the woman asked her friends for advice concerning Andrei's inability to have sex. Rumors spread swiftly, as Chikatilo later told police: "Girls were going behind my back, whispering that I was impotent. I was so ashamed. I tried to hang myself. My mother and some young neighbors pulled me out of the noose. Well, I thought no one would want such a shamed man. So I had to run away from there, away from my homeland."

He landed in Rostov-on-Don, a port city and the administrative center of Rostov Oblast and of

Russia's Southern Federal District, situated on the Don River, 20 miles from the Sea of Azov. Sister Tatyana finished school in 1961 and moved in with Andrei for six months, then married a local boy and transferred to her in-laws' home. Before long, their parents also moved to Rostov-on-Don, and Tatyana set about finding a mate for her older brother. In 1963, she settled on Feodosia Odnacheva, introducing her to Andrei and driving the relationship forward until they married only two weeks after meeting for the first time. A normal sex life still eluded Andrei, but Feodosia finally agreed they should have children by means of Andrei ejaculating in his hand, then shoving the semen inside her. By that odd means they managed to conceive a daughter, Lyudmila, in 1965, and a son, Yuri, four years later.

Meanwhile, Chikatilo needed a steady source of income. In 1965 he began a five-year correspondence course in Russian literature from Rostov's Southern Federal University, managing regional sports activities on the side until he obtained his degree in 1970. A newly licensed teacher, he found a classroom vacancy in Novoshakhtinsk, near Rostov Oblast's border with Ukraine, but his unruly students regularly mocked him, prompting a transfer to Technical School No. 33 in Shakhty, 47 miles northeast of Rostov-on-Don.

The change of scene only made Chikatilo's problems worse. In May 1973, while swimming, he grabbed and fondled a 15-year-old girl, ejaculating as she struggled with him. Several months later, he attacked another teenager whom he had locked in his classroom. On yet another occasion, fellow teachers saw Chikatilo fondling himself with students present, and he allegedly entered girls' dormitory rooms repeatedly, hoping to catch them undressed.

Communist Party membership had its privileges, sparing Chikatilo from censure in those early cases, but complaints soon grew too numerous to be ignored. In December 1974, the school's director offered him a choice or resigning or being fired. Chikatilo took the easy route, and soon found another teaching position in Novoshakhtinsk the following month. Staff reductions cost him that job in September 1978, but he moved on to another school in Shakhty. There, complaints resumed of Andrei sexually assaulting both male and female students, leading to his last dismissal as a teacher in March 1981.

By that time, he had killed his first victim, nine-year-old Yelena Zakotnova. Chikatilo found her walking home from an ice skating rink in Shakhty, luring her to an abandoned house he had secretly purchased. There, he attacked and tried to rape Yelena, but failed to achieve an erection, whereupon he choked her and stabbed her three times, finally ejaculating as the knife pierced her abdomen. Afterward, he tossed her corpse from a bridge into the Grushevka River, where hikers found it on Christmas Eve.

Police had ample evidence to work with: blood found on the snow near Chikatilo's secret hideaway, testimony from neighbors who saw him there on December 22, and an eyewitness description of a man closely resembling Chikatilo whom the witness saw with Zakotnova at a bus stop the same afternoon. Nonetheless, detectives arrested 25-year-old Aleksandr Kravchenko, who had served time for raping and killing another girl as a teenager. Their case came down to spots of blood found on a jumper owned by

Kravchenko's wife, its type matching both hers and the victim's. Kravchenko's wife and a friend provided his alibi, verified by neighbors, placing him at home during the crime, but Kravchenko's wife changed her tune when officers threatened to charge her as an accessory to murder. Kravchenko, in despair, confessed, then recanted at trial in 1979. He received a death sentence, later commuted to 15 years — Russia's longest permissible prison term at the time — but pressure from Zakotnova's family prompted a new trial, where the death sentence was reinstated. Kravchenko was executed for Chikatilo's crime in July 1983.

By that time, Yelena Zakotnova's slayer had claimed 10 more victims

Only days after his final dismissal as a teacher, Chikatilo found work as a supply clerk at a Rostov factory for construction materials. The job required extensive travel, negotiating supply contracts and purchasing raw materials. His marriage remained a sexual wasteland, with Andrei stymied by arousal short of lethal violence. He struggled to resist that urge, but it was all consuming, irresistible.

He struck again on September 3, 1981, spotting 17-year-old Larisa Tkachenko at a bus stop as Chikatilo left a public library in downtown Rostov. Larisa was waiting for a ride back to her boarding school, but she accepted his invitation to drink vodka and "relax" in woodlands near the Don River. Arriving there, Andrei threw her down and tore at her clothing, beating, strangling, and suffocating Larisa with a mouthful of mud when she resisted. Caught without a knife that time, he bit off one nipple, further mutilated her body with a stick, then covered her with foliage and old newspaper pages, a ruse that failed to conceal her from a passer-by the next day.

On June 12, 1982, Chikatilo snatched 13-year-old Lyubov Biryuk as she returned home from Donskoy, a town in Tula Oblast, located on the upper stream of the Don River. Chikatilo had been grocery shopping in Rostov's Bagayevsky District and decided to walk home after changing buses at Donskoy. They fell into conversation while Andrei watched for witnesses, then he leapt upon her and stabbed her 22 times, also gouging out both eyes with his blade. Her corpse was found on June 27.

Casting discretion to the wind, Chikatilo killed six more victims in as many months: 14-year-old Lyubov Volobuyeva, slain in an orchard near Krasnodar International Airport, 92 miles northeast of the Black Sea port of Novorossiysk, on July 25, found August 7; nine-year-old Oleg Pozhidayev, Andrei's first male victim, murdered at Adygea in the foothills of the Northwestern Caucasus, never recovered; Olga Kuprina, a 16-year-old runaway from Semikarakorsky District in Rostov Oblast, killed at Kazachi Lagerya on August 16 and found October 27; 18-year-old Irina Karabelnikova, lured from Shakhty's railway station on September 8, found 12 days later; another boy, 15-year-old Sergey Kuzmin, killed near Shakhty station after absconding from boarding school, found on January 12, 1983; and 10-year-old Olga Stalmachenok, who met Chikatilo on a bus, stabbed more than 50 times in a cornfield near Novoshakhtinsk, with her uterus and lower bowel cut out.

Postmortem examination showed each victim was beaten and choked before stabbing and mutilation occurred, most found with their eyes cut out. Some were bound before the slaughter commenced. Afterward, in custody, Andrei admitted luring each in turn with offers of food or sweets, vodka or money, even a chance to see rare coins, stamps, or films. His efforts to conceal the bodies were clumsy and rarely successful.

By January 1983, with four victims linked to one "pattern" killer, Major Mikhail Fetisov arrived in Rostov-on-Don, directing a team of 10 detectives augmented by forensics expert Viktor Burakov, but Communist Party officials still rejected the notion of a serial killer at large in the USSR, demanding that investigators focus on psychiatric patients, homosexuals, pedophiles, even satanic cultists or outlaw organ harvesters. Several young men with mental disabilities muddied the waters by confessing to various murders, typically after long and brutal interrogations, and three innocent gay suspects were convicted of individual slayings at trial. Even so, the ongoing manhunt legitimately solved more than 1,000 unrelated crimes, including 95 murders and 245 rapes.

And still the slayings continued, with Procurator General of the USSR Alexander Rekunkov officially linking six victims to the same unknown killer by September 6, 1983. But Chikatilo had not finished killing.

After a six-month hiatus, his next victim was 15-year-old Laura Sarkisyan, an Armenian runaway slain in the forest near an unmarked railway platform outside Shakhty on June 18, 1983. Andrei named her in his final confession but was still acquitted of her murder. Others included 13-year-old Irina Dunenkova, a mentally handicapped student killed on July 13, found at Rostov's Aviators' Park on August 8;

Lyudmila Kutsyuba, a homeless mother of two, slain near a Shakhty bus station on July 24, found on March 12, 1984; Andrei's youngest victim and another boy, seven-year-old Igor Gudkov, killed at Aviators' Park on August 9; an unidentified woman Andrei described as a prostitute, taken from a Novoshakhtinsk bus station sometime between July 18 and August 25, found on October 8; 22-year-old Valentina Chuchulina, murdered sometime after September 19 and found near Kirpichnaya railway station on November 27; and 19-year-old Vera Shevkun, killed at a mining village near Shakhty, found three days later.

And the bloody toll continued into 1984: 14-year-old Sergey Markov, abducted while walking home from work experience training, found near Novocherkassk on January 4; 17-year-old Natalya Shalapinina, a close friend of victim Olga Kuprina, slain at Aviators' Park on January 9; another victim from Aviators' Park, 44-year-old Marta Ryabenko, killed on February 21 and found the next day; 10-year-old Dmitriy Ptashnikov, lured from a Novoshakhtinsk stamp kiosk on March 24; 29-year-old Tatyana Petrosyan, acquainted with Chikatilo since 1978, slain with her daughter Svetlana outside Shakhty on May 25; 21-year-old Yelena Bakulina, killed in Rostov's Bagasenski district on June 22, found August 7; 13-year-old Dmitriy Illarionov, missing from Rostov on July 10, found in a cornfield on August 12; 19-year-old Anna Lemesheva, killed near Kirpichnaya railway station after a dental appointment on July 19; 20-year-old Sarmite Tsana, killed around July 28 and found on September 9 at Aviators' Park; 16-year-old Natalya Golosovskaya, killed at Aviators' Park on August 2; 17-year-old Lyudmila Alekseyeva, lured away from

Rostov's bus terminal on August 7; an unidentified woman, aged 20 to 25, met by Chikatilo on a business trip to the Uzbek Soviet Socialist Republic between August 8 and 11, found August 16; Akmaral Seydaliyeva, a 10-year-old runaway from Alma-Ata, Kazakhstan, killed in Tashkent, Uzbek SSR on August 13; 11-year-old Aleksandr Chepel, killed August 28 on the banks of the Don River, near the Alekseyeva murder scene, found September 2; and Rostov librarian Irina Luchinskaya, age 24, killed at Aviators' Park while en route to a sauna on September 6.

One week after Luchinskaya's murder, an undercover detective saw Chikatilo trying to lure young women away from Rostov's bus station. When detained for questioning, Andrei carried a knife and a length of rope concealed on his person. Police learned that he was also under investigation for theft from a previous employer, examined his prior accusations of child molestation, and found a witness whose description of Dmitry Ptashnikov's killer matched Chikatilo. Confusion arose concerning his blood type — A — because semen samples from six "Ripper" victims apparently came from a type AB secretor. By that time, the Rostov murder file listed 25,000 suspects, and the Procurator General linked 23 victims to a single killer. Charges were dropped against the addled youths who had falsely confessed, and Chikatilo was finally convicted only on one count of theft, sentenced to a year in prison, then released on December 12, 1984.

He emerged to find new work at a locomotive factory in Novocherkassk, suppressing his homicidal urges for eight months. On August 1, 1985, he broke cover, killing 18-year-old Natalya Pokhlistova near

Domodedovo Airport in Moscow Oblast. Her body was found two days later. On August 27, Chikatilo struck again, murdering 18-year-old Irina Gulyayeva in woodlands near Shakhty's bus station, her corpse found the following day.

In November 1985, Moscow assigned special procurator Issa Kostoyev to supervise the Ripper manhunt, with a task force expanded to include 15 subordinate procurators and 29 detectives. Police patrols of railway stations surrounding Rostov-on-Don intensified, with plainclothes female officers staked out as bait. Meanwhile, Viktor Burakov hired consulting psychiatrist Alexandr Bukhanovsky to prepare the Soviet Union's first-ever profile of an unidentified serial killer. Dr. Bukhanovsky's 65-page report described a man aged 45 to 50, likely married with children, although plagued by impotence except when he saw victims suffer, substituting homicide for normal intercourse. Murders committed on weekdays, near mass transit hubs, suggested a slayer tied to a strict production schedule.

Chikatilo, following the manhunt from newspaper clippings, apparently suppressed his lust for blood over the next 21 months—or, at least, he more skillfully covered his tracks. No more corpses with signature mutilations surfaced in Rostov or Moscow Oblasts during that time, although police suspected their unknown subject of two crimes in the summer of 1986. On July 23, officers found 33-year-old Lyubov Golovakha stabbed more than 20 times in Rostov's Myasnikovsky District, and while the killer's semen matched a type AB secretor, she did not bear the Ripper's trademark mutilations. On August 18, workers found 18-year-old secretary Irina Pogoryelova buried on a collective farm at Bataysk, Rostov Oblast, slashed from neck to groin, one breast removed, and her eyes gouged out. That murder fit the bill, but investigators remained divided, some suspecting a copycat, while others thought the original killer was taking more pains to conceal his victims. By autumn 1986, some officers believed the killer had moved on to new hunting grounds or might have been arrested and imprisoned on some unrelated charge.

But Chikatilo was not gone, merely biding his time, and in 1987, he returned with a vengeance. On May 16 he killed 12-year-old Oleg Makarenkov, a boarding school student slain in Revda, Sverdlovsk Oblast, leading police to the boy's grave after his arrest. July 29 saw 12-year-old Ivan Bilovetsky slain along a railway line near Zaporizhia in Ukraine, found by his own father the next day. On September 15, Chikatilo lured 16-year-old Yuri Tereshonok to his death from a train in Leningrad, later leading police to his corpse.

Three more victims died in 1988. An unidentified woman, age 22 to 28, fell prey between April 1 and 4, found on April 6 where Chikatilo dumped her, on the grounds of a metal factory near Krasny Sulin railway station, Rostov Oblast. On May 15, while on a business trip to Artyomovsk, a town 110 miles south of Krasnoyarsk, Krasnoyarsk Krai, Andrei met nine-year-old Aleksey Voronko and killed him at Ilovaisk, Ukraine. Two months later, on July 14, Andrei murdered 15-year-old Yevgeniy Muratov near Rostov, found at Donleskhoz railway station on April 10, 1989.

The year 1989 claimed five more victims: Tatyana Ryzhova, a 16-year-old runaway from Krasny

Sulin, Rostov Oblast, slain and dismembered in the apartment of Andrei's own daughter on March 1, her remains found eight days later; Aleksandr Dyakonov, killed in shrubbery near downtown Rostov on May 11 — one day after his eighth birthday — and found July 14; 10-year-old Aleksey Moiseyev, described by Andrei to police as "a boy from Kolchugino, Vladimir Oblast, whom I took from the beach into the forest"; 19-year-old Yelena Varga, a Hungarian student and single mother, tempted from a bus and slain on August 19, at a village near Rostov-on-Don; and 10-year-old Aleksey Khobotov, encountered by Chikatilo outside a Shakhty theater and buried at a local cemetery, his grave revealed to police after Andrei's arrest.

Even as time ran out for Chikatilo in 1990, he kept killing, and his first murder for the year was nearly a replay of 1989's last, claiming 11-year-old Andrei Kravchenko from a street near his Shakhty home on January 14, his emasculated body found in nearby woodland on February 19. Ten-year-old Yaroslav Makarov was next to die, on March 7, taken from a Rostov railway station while playing hooky from school, found the next day with his tongue and genitals removed. On April 4, 31-year-old Lyubov Zuyeva met Chikatilo on a train traveling from Novocherkassk to Shakhty, lured off to her death at Donleskhoz station. Andrei killed 13-year-old Viktor Petrov on July 28, dumping his corpse a few yards from the Makarov crime scene, at Rostov's botanical gardens. Ivan Fomin, age 11, met his fate at Novocherkassk's municipal beach, stabbed 42 times and emasculated, found three days later. On October 17, Vadim Gromov, a 16-year-old handicapped student from Shakhty, vanished from a train bound for

Taganrog, Rostov Oblast, his murder later confessed to by Chikatilo. Viktor Tishchenko, age 16, fought grimly for his life in Shakhty on October 30, biting and breaking one of Andrei's fingers. Finally, on November 6, Chikatilo murdered Svetlana Korostik, a 22-year-old homeless woman, in the woods near Donleskhoz station, her corpse found seven days later.

Discovery of new, confirmed victims reinvigorated the Ripper manhunt. Switching tactics, on October 27 Viktor Burakov sent 360 uniformed police swarming over most of the railway stations in Rostov Oblast, posting plainclothes officers only at the three smallest stations: Donleskhoz, Kirpichnaya, and Lesostep. After eleven watchful days, on November 6, an undercover cop saw Chikatilo leave the woods near Donleskhoz station where he had just killed Svetlana Korostik, pausing to wash his hands and face at a well. Unaware of the crime, the officer noted a red smudge on Andrei's cheek, plus grass and oil stains on his jacket. The officer checked his I.D. but had no reason to detain him, filing a routine report upon his return to headquarters.

When Korostik's remains surfaced one week later, a review of reports from the Donleskhoz station turned up a familiar name: Andrei Chikatilo, questioned in 1984 and added to a suspect list circulated nationwide three years later. Interviews with past and present employers placed Andrei near other murder sites, and again his record of dismissal as a teacher returned to haunt him. Officers mounted surveillance on Andrei from November 14 onward, observing several failed attempts to strike up conversations with lone children and young women.

Six days later, officers arrested Chikatilo outside a café in Novocherkassk and drove him to jail.

As in 1984, Andrei he was found armed with a knife and lengths of rope, but he initially denied everything. Examination in custody revealed his injured finger, broken and with the nail bitten off by victim Viktor Tishchenko. Next, the anomaly of his blood type was resolved by revelation that in rare cases, a person may secrete one blood type with saliva and a different type with semen, which proved true in Chikatilo's case. At last, with only hours left before Russian law mandated he be charged or released, Dr. Bukhanovsky confronted Chikatilo with his psychological profile, and the Ripper broke down in tears, confessing his crimes through that night and on subsequent days. Every detail from his memory matched the wounds found on victims he dismissed as "déclassé elements" unworthy of life. He had blinded victims, Andrei said, from the belief that a corpse's eyes retained images of their killer. He also admitted acts akin to cannibalism: chewing on one victim's uterus and another's testicles, swallowing nipples from several. At such times, Andrei said, he "felt chills" and "shook all over."

Police finished their interrogation, including crime scene reenactments, on August 20, 1991. Next came psychiatrists, judging Chikatilo's fitness for trial at Moscow's Serbsky State Scientific Center for Social and Forensic Psychiatry. Dr. Andrei Tkachenko granted that Chikatilo suffered physiological problems attributed to prenatal brain damage, along with borderline personality disorder and sadistic features, but still found him legally sane for purposes of trial.

That trial commenced in Rostov-on-Don, on April 14, 1992, including 53 murder counts and five charges related to child molestation committed as a teacher, years before. Chikatilo arrived in court with his head shaved, to foil prison lice, confined inside a tempered glass box to prevent spectators from attacking him. He mugged for press cameras and barked gibberish until Judge Leonid Akubzhanov snapped, "Shut your mouth! You're not crazy." On other occasions, Andrei exposed himself in court or sang random snatches of Socialist ballads while his audience jeered. Judge Akubzhanov denied the defense attorney's motion for another psychiatric test, and replaced prosecutor Nikolai Gerasimenko for supporting that petition. Closing arguments began on August 9, and Judge Akubzhanov convicted Chikatilo of 52 murder counts, plus the five ancient counts of sexual assault, on October 14. One day later, Andrei received a death sentence for each of the capital charges, plus 86 years in prison.

The Supreme Court of the Soviet Union denied Chikatilo's appeal, followed by a thumbs-down from President Boris Yeltsin on January 4, 1994. Six weeks later, on February 14, guards led Chikatilo from his death row cell at Novocherkassk prison to a soundproof chamber, where an executioner killed him with a point-blank pistol shot behind his right ear.

10. Sergey Golovkin: "The Fisher"

Psychiatrists frequently argue the impact of birth defects on future serial killers. A name often raised in such debates is Sergey Aleksandrovich Golovkin, born in Moscow on November 26, 1959. His father was a brutal alcoholic, his mother uncommunicative to the point of silence in their home, finally divorced from Sergey's father in 1988. Golovkin was born with a defective sternum — breastbone — which caused him to stand and walk with slumped shoulders, also making him a frequent victim of bronchitis and indigestion. Adding insult to injury, he was also a chronic bed wetter, who entered school fearing his classmates would notice a stench of urine about him. His drunken father sought to purge that problem with "water procedures," repeatedly dumping ice-cold water on his son, but it had the reverse effect, prompting Sergey to shun baths.

Preludes to murder? Not necessarily. And yet...

At Moscow Secondary School No. 167, Golovkin developed a loner's reputation, male peers noting that he seemed to have no interest in girls. His classmates included Armen Grigoryan, Alexander Sevostyanov and Igor Shuldinger, founders of the rock group *Krematorij* ("Crematorium"), organized in 1983 and still active today, but the future stars harbor no memories of Golovkin. Others recall his poor personal hygiene — likely engendered by his father's "water procedures" at home — and his habit of smoking cigarette butts he retrieved from the streets. After his arrest, former classmate Golovkina Slobodin later told reporters, "The girls liked the guys well dressed and carried away by the music. And he was stooped, pimpled and no one paid attention to him."

In fact, Golovkin's disinterest in girls seemed to be innate. By age 13, in 1972, he was enjoying full-blown sadistic fantasies and sometimes acting them out, as when he snatched a neighbor's cat and brought it home to behead it and hang it in his yard. From that event, he later said, "came the discharge, a feeling of power, and mental relief." Increasingly, while masturbating, he imagined having intercourse with classmates, then torturing them and burning them at the stake. Another of his dreams involved "the exhumation of a corpse and dismemberment." From there, it was a short step to imagining himself as one of Adolf Hitler's Nazis, torturing and executing fellow Russians during wartime. Increasingly, the objects of his grisly dreams and fantasies transformed from animals to slender teenage boys, Golovkin's sexual obsession for the rest of his life.

Still, he maintained an avid interest in other species, graduating in 1982 from Moscow's Timiryazev Agricultural Academy, established in 1865, named for botanist and physiologist Kliment Timiryazev (1843-1920). From there, he found work at a racetrack, then at a Moscow stud farm. In 1989, his achievements in horse breeding earned Golovkin a silver medal at the Vystavka Dostizheniy Narodnogo Khozyaystva ("Exhibition of Achievements of National Economy"), a permanent general-purpose trade show and amusement park in Moscow.

Golovkin seemed well on his way to a stellar career in livestock breeding, but he harbored a dark secret. Five years before winning the VDNKh silver medal, in 1984, he had already botched his first attempt at murder, raping a 17-year-old boy who escaped his clutches after the assault. Police failed to identify him in that case, and he resolved to do better next time.

Golovkin carried out his first successful slaying in April 1986, near the Katuar railway station in Nekrasov, Moscow Oblast, a hub for commuter trains serving the Russian capital. Victim Andrey Pavlov was 15 years old, terrified when Golovkin pulled a knife and threatened him, then dragged him into nearby woods, where he raped Pavlov, then strangled him to death and finally ravaged his corpse, expanding his repertoire to include necrophilia.

Three months later, Golovkin struck again, kidnapping 12-year-old Andrey Gulyaev from a summer camp near Odintsovo, the administrative center of Moscow Oblast's Odintsovsky District. As before, Golovkin held his prey at knifepoint, conveyed him into nearby woods, then raped and strangled Gulyaev before emasculating, disemboweling, and dismembering his corpse.

Murder was pleasurable for Golovkin, but he recognized the need for a secure location, safe from unexpected discovery. In 1988 he bought a used VAZ-2103 "deluxe" compact sedan, patterned on Italy's Fiat 124 Special, manufactured under license for the Soviet and Eastern European market. Golovkin housed the car in his garage, where he immediately started excavation of a basement, ostensibly intended as an ordinary workshop, soon transformed into a torture dungeon for his future prey.

Between August 1990 and September 1992, Golovkin killed eight boys, aged 10 to 15, in his secret dungeon. In one case, he hung his victim, then suspended the corpse upside-down before mutilating it from head to toe, excising ears, nose, and genitals, finally cracking the boy's skull to remove and burn his brain. Golovkin also sampled the victim's flesh, but was put off by its taste and thereafter left cannibalism to others with stronger stomachs. Instead, he began to keep trophies removed from the corpses, including a large patch of skin which he flayed from one victim, preserving it with salt.

On two occasions, Golovkin brought home pairs of victims to his dungeon, torturing each in turn while the other looked on, then killing them one at a time. He later told police that in such cases, the last to die appeared to take his friend's death and dismemberment "with odd calmness" that bemused Golovkin. Finally, in September 1992, he procured three young victims at once, enticing them with a scheme to rob a warehouse. Once sequestered in the basement, they were trapped, the last of them surviving 12 hours of rape and torture before he expired. Mushroom pickers found the last three corpses dumped together, on October 5.

Police in Moscow Oblast knew a killer was at work within their jurisdiction, but geography conspired for a time to shield Golovkin from suspicion. Specifically, while his garage and dungeon were located near the rural stud farm where he worked, Golovkin's registered address was in Moscow proper, initially casting him as an unlikely suspect. Detained for questioning on October 19, 1992, Golovkin seemed calm and collected, denying any criminal activity.

Justice Eugene Bakin and a homicide inspector named Kostarëv planned to release him while keeping him under surveillance, but a jailer misunderstood the order and held Golovkin overnight in solitary confinement. The next morning, when questioned again, he cracked at once and confessed his three most recent homicides. A search of his garage turned up copious evidence of other slayings, and Golovkin finally confessed to 11 murders overall.

State psychiatrists examined Golovkin, pronouncing him schizophrenic but legally sane by Soviet standards. At trial, where reading of Golovkin's 95-page indictment consumed several hours, the defense could not explain away the grisly relics retrieved from his garage, nor rebut the testimony of Golovkin's surviving rape victim from 1984. Convicted of all counts on October 19, 1994, Golovkin received a death sentence. Shot by a uniformed executioner on August 2, 1996, he remains the last prisoner executed before Russia imposed its moratorium on capital punishment.

As Golovkin's memory fades from public consciousness in Moscow, doubt still surrounds the nicknames with which reporters tagged him. There seems to be no basis for the "Fisher" sobriquet, despite one published mention of "tattoos," though it may refer to his method of stalking victims. Justice Eugene Bakin apparently took credit for an alternate nickname — "The Boa" — by comparing Golovkin's cold-blooded methods to those of a South American boa constrictor. To the very end, Bakin recalled, Golovkin voiced no remorse for his crimes, still "considering himself a superman, that all is permitted."

11. Vasiliy Kulik: "The Irkutsk Monster"

One Internet website declares, in an epic understatement, that "Vasiliy Kulik, better known as 'The Irkutsk Monster,' was not a very nice man." He was not simply volatile or foul-tempered, however, but in fact a serial slayer of 13 victims, whose chosen prey waffled from children to elderly victims, aged between seven months and 75 years.

Nothing in Kulik's family prepared them for the private holocaust he would unleash in later life. He was born in Irkutsk Oblast, southeastern Siberia, on January 17, 1956, youngest of three children produced by the union of Sergei Kulik, a doctor of biological sciences and an author, while his mother was a public school headmistress. Neither had a blemish to their names; all published sources agree that his parents were "decent and respected," one going so far as to dub them "nobles."

In Vasily's case, however, the apple fell far from its paternal trees. From childhood, he was a sleepwalker who displayed a morbid fascination with violence and sex, torturing animals and swaggering about in an exaggerated parody of "macho" male behavior, striving to appear as "a strong man." Part of that image proved true in secondary school, where Kulik enjoyed boxing, became Irkutsk's city champion in his age class, and enjoyed the company of "many girlfriends." None of the relationships proved to be durable, however, and the one he seemed to treasure most ended abruptly when the girl's family left Irkutsk, plunging Kulik into deep depression. Years later, his two older sisters recalled him as selfish and cruel.

Another, contrasting view of Vasiliy's adolescence came later, from his mother, after his arrest. She remembered her son as physically weak and walking with a limp, mentally unstable and attempting suicide when his father died unexpectedly. Be that as it may, he qualified for military service in 1974, at age 18, and served two full years in the Soviet Army. Following his discharge, Kulik enrolled at the Irkutsk Medical Institute, hoping to become a physician. During that time, he attempted to seduce numerous women, both fellow students and wives of older men, but rejection came to him more often than success. In due time, he married a lawyer who bore him two or three sons (reports differ).

In 1980, he was robbed and beaten by a gang of young muggers, suffering head trauma that curtailed his medical education. Stopping well short of a medical degree, he graduated as a medic in 1982 and found work at Irkutsk Station Emergency, an ambulance service, administering first-aid to accident victims. Long afterward, he said of his attack, "For the last five or six years [since his head injury], I regularly visited the thoughts of a sexual nature, where I perform sexual acts with children. At first, I was only thinking about the girls, and then about the boys, as well as the old women."

In short, he had acquired the traits of both a predatory pedophile, sexually drawn to children, and those of a gerontophile, fixated on the elderly. Before year's end of 1980, he penned the manuscript for a novel detailing his imaginary seduction of a nine-year-old girl. That "literary" work never went to press, and Kulik's mental state steadily degenerated. Between 1984 and 1986 he eschewed all self-restraint, attacking and killing a total of 13 known victims.

Like most fledgling serial killers, however, Kulik worked his way up to murder by stages. Poring over records at his workplace, he acquired the addresses of former patients with young children, broke into their homes, and raped their offspring, either male or female. According to the Russian media, "very few" of those attacks were mentioned to police during the time when they occurred. None of those early victims died, though we can only speculate upon the trauma they endured in later life.

Kulik committed his first murder in 1984, selecting an elderly woman whom he drugged with supplies from his job at Irkutsk Station Emergency, plunging her into unconsciousness. From there, he raped and strangled her, although her death was blamed on coronary artery disease—also called ischemic heart disease—in fact a group of ailments including both stable and unstable angina (chest pains), myocardial infarction (commonly called a heart attack, inducing tissue death of the heart muscles), and sudden cardiac death without prior warnings.

For his second victim, Kulik targeted an eight-year-old girl who fought him energetically but failed to save herself. In his third attack, he shot, then stabbed a 53-year-old woman. His other victims, picked erratically, included six children between the ages of seven months and two years, plus seven elderly women. His oldest adult victim was aged 73 or 75 (again, published accounts vary).

Kulik's luck ran out on January 17, 1986 — ironically, his 30th birthday. The victim chosen for that twisted celebration proved too much for him, beating and stabbing Kulik into submission before she summoned police. In custody, The Monster of Irkutsk proved affable enough with his interrogators, confessing a series of crimes that included 13 murders, plus nearly 30 more nonfatal rapes and assaults committed during his two-year rampage.

Psychiatrists, as usual, found Kulik sane and fit for trial within the limits of Soviet law. On August 11, 1988, the Irkutsk Oblast Court convicted him on all outstanding counts of his indictment and imposed a death sentence. While his appeals dragged on, going nowhere, Kulik maintained a civilized façade in prison, writing poetry and granting media interviews in which he ruminated on the nature of life and death. Some published accounts claim Kulik was executed without public notice, his death virtually hushed up by authorities, but more authoritative sources say he was dispatched on June 26, 1989, by a lone executioner who fired one pistol shot into his brain.

12. Alexander Spesivtsev: "The Novokuznetsk Monster"

Some killers, after being captured, pad their criminal résumés by confessing to numerous crimes they did not commit. In certain cases, negligent police are glad to clear their books by feeding suspects details from their cold case files; in others, boastful suspects may fabricate details of murders detectives can neither confirm nor deny, based on lack of evidence. Alexander Spesivtsev may be one such braggart, but authorities remain uncertain. Convicted of four homicides, he confessed to another 19 from police open files, and detectives suspect him of more than 80 — many committed with the aid of his loving mother.

Alexander Nikolayevich Spesivtsev was born on March 1, 1970, in Novokuznetsk, a major coal mining and industrial center in southwestern Siberia's Kemerovo Oblast. Harsh winters are the rule in Novokuznetsk, where temperatures often fall below -40 degrees Fahrenheit. Still, more than half a million people inhabit the city today, pursuing livelihoods interspersed with diversions provided by the Kontinental Hockey League and Professional Rugby League.

Underweight at birth and often ill thereafter, frequently abused by his violent father, Spesivtsev had no interest in sports and little more in making friends. He was standoffish, often targeted by bullies, and drew whatever consolation he could find from mother Lyudmila, a city school employee who seemingly reserved all her affection for young Alexander in a bonding that police would later label "strong but unusual." They shared a bed until Alexander was 12 years old, their cuddling interspersed with Lyudmila showing her son — nicknamed "Sasha" — photographs of corpses from various true-crime books. By age 18, Alexander's budding sadism was pronounced enough to rate him an in-patient term at a Novokuznetsk psychiatric hospital, which accomplished precisely nothing.

Soviet communism collapsed three years later, in 1991, increasing the amount of poverty in Novokuznetsk. Particularly noticeable was a free-floating population of homeless street children, whom Spesivtsev and his mother disdained as "the detritus of society." Reports differ as to when they took a personal approach to curbing the problem, but all agree that mother and son began luring children home to their downtown apartment on Pionerskiy Prospekt. Alexander's father had departed by that time, leaving the flat to his ex-wife and son, with their Doberman pinscher watchdog.

Once inside the Spesivtsev apartment, there was no escape for young victims selected at random. Each in turn was tortured, then stabbed to death and dismembered, parts of their remains devoured by Alexander, Lyudmila, and their Doberman. Unwanted bits were kept for disposal late at night, when Lyudmila left the flat and tossed them into the Aba River, which meets and merges with the larger Tom River near Novokuznetsk, bearing rich coal deposits. Recovery of mutilated remains from the Aba alerted police to a killer in their midst, but they still had no idea who that might be or where to look.

Over the years of killing, Alexander kept a diary detailing 19 of his crimes but may have omitted others for reasons best known to himself. He also found time to acquire a girlfriend, although his Gothic lifestyle doomed their relationship from the onset. Though she can scarcely have missed the grim evidence decorating Spesivtsev's apartment, she kept silent until Alexander felt the risk too great and added her to his growing list of corpses.

The cannibals' last victims comprised a young female threesome, lured to the flat on Pionerskiy Prospekt under the pretext of shifting some clutter. Once they were inside, Alexander attacked all three, beating and raping them, killing one with his knife, then forcing the survivors to dismember their friend in his family's bathtub, before Lyudmila served parts of her corpse as a bizarre last supper. After that ghastly meal, Alexander set his Doberman on another of the girls, watching it maul her to death. Finally, he shoved the last survivor, 15-year-old Olga Galtseva, onto the couch and plunged his blade repeatedly into her body.

At that point, fate or dumb luck intervened. A water pipe burst in the apartment house and neighbors called a plumber, who traced the leak back to the Spesivtsevs' flat. When no one answered his knock, he forced the door open, then instantly recoiled and ran to call police. Alexander, meanwhile, had heard the door open, leaping from the apartment's balcony and fleeing on foot.

First responders to the scene found Olga Galtseva bleeding on the couch and called an ambulance, together with detectives. Moving through the flat, they saw bloodstains across the walls, bowls in the kitchen filled with human remains, a rib cage in the living room, Alexander's confessional diary, and a headless, mutilated girl's corpse in the bathtub. Other items recovered included 82 articles of bloody clothing, 40 pieces of stolen jewelry and numerous photographs, many of persons never identified. Olga Galtseva lived for another 17 hours, briefing police on her last night of horror, before she expired from blood loss and internal damage.

In retrospect, police admitted that their manhunt for the cannibals of Novokuznetsk had become a tragic comedy of errors, fueled at least in part by budget woes that plagued the whole Russian bureaucracy after the USSR fell apart in 1991. As in the Chikatilo case and others worldwide, police placed a low priority on finding lost street children, if the victims were even reported missing, a combination of apathy and ingrained prejudice. Researching case files proved embarrassing, as neighbors of the Spevitsevs had complained of foul smells emanating from their apartment, accompanied by deafening rock music, but police dismissed those calls as a simple feud, not worth their time investigating. Even after bodies were recovered from the flat, detectives blamed lack of funds for a failure to search the apartment house grounds.

Stories differ as to how the cannibal mother and son were arrested, doubtless confounded by the East-West language barrier. Some reports claim Alexander remained at large until he invaded a stranger's apartment, trying to rape her, and police showed up to catch him in the act. Others simply state that he and Lyudmila were jailed together on October 26, 1996, without reference to any unusual circumstances. The Doberman's fate goes unmentioned, but animals in such cases are normally euthanized.

As trial approached, Kemerovo Oblast Procurator Alexei Bugayets was confident of convicting Alexander for the 19 murders listed in his private diary. Based on translated stories online, it appears that Alexander *was* convicted and sentenced to die, but on appeal was judged to be insane and transferred to the familiar confines of a psychiatric institution in Kamyshin, Volgograd Oblast, on October 5, 1999. Mother Lyudmila, for her part, rolled the dice with a not guilty plea and lost out, sentenced to life in prison.

At his new institutional home, Alexander spends most of his time on psychiatric interviews, and has allegedly penned several unpublished manuscripts on philosophy, stockpiled by keepers who describe him as "an intellectual." Sometimes he justifies his crimes, rhetorically asking interviewers, "How many people have our democracy destroyed? If people thought about that, there wouldn't be any of this filth [homeless children]. But what can you do?" At his eventual death, he claims to hope some institution will purchase his head for further study. The price: payment "in advance, in cigarettes."

13. Alexander Pichushkin: "The Chessboard Killer"

Russia's "silver medalist" serial killer, officially standing in second place behind Andrei Chikatilo (Chapter 9) for a confirmed body count, presents the case of an outwardly normal person whose mind and life changed radically following a childhood head trauma. Whether that, in fact, explains his crimes remains a subject of debate among penologists, psychologists, and others fascinated by the grim phenomenon of random murder.

Alexander Yuryevich Pichushkin, nicknamed "Sasha" from his youth, was born in Moscow on April 9, 1974, the son of an alcoholic father who abandoned the family when Sasha was an infant. An "initially sociable child," he fell backwards from a swing at age four, then was struck in the forehead as the swing rebounded. Some physicians speculate that the blow damaged his brain's frontal cortex, the portion associated with aggressiveness and impulse control. And indeed, soon afterward, Pichushkin frequently became hostile without apparent reason, prompting his mother to remove him from his mainstream school, away from bullies who scorned him as "that retard," in favor of a special school for children with learning disabilities.

A drawback of that school was its primary emphasis on overcoming disabilities, rather than promoting scholastic achievement. With the onset of adolescence, Pichushkin's maternal grandparents pegged him as intelligent and took him into their home, encouraging pursuit of intellectual activities such as chess. Alexander displayed a talent for the game, moving on to exhibition matches against elderly men who gathered to play at Bitsevski Park, in southwestern Moscow. The game, the locale, and his early opponents all assumed significance in Pichushkin's later career as a serial killer.

A second blow rocked Alexander's world when his grandfather died, forcing him back to his mother's home. Pichushkin regarded the old man's death as a betrayal and abandonment, further fueling his anger at elderly opponents who had faced him across a chessboard. While the exhibition games continued, with Pichushkin normally victorious, he began to drink large quantities of vodka, which apparently did not affect his game.

Around the same time, the future "Bitsevski Park Maniac" acquired a video camera, carrying it with him while he threatened younger children and taped their fearful reactions. On one such tape, he clutched a sobbing victim by the leg, lifting him upside-down while saying, "You are in my power now. I am going to drop you from the window and you will fall 15 meters to your death."

By age 18, in 1992, mere threats no longer sated Pichushkin's urges. He needed more, and in October of that year he found an idol in the person of "Rostov Ripper" Andrei Chikatilo, convicted and sentenced to die for 52 murders. It would be grand, Pichushkin thought, to surpass Chikatilo's tally — and why not make it 64 victims, matching the number of squares on a chessboard? Later, he recanted his confession of that goal, admitting that his crimes would have continued regardless of numbers, until he was finally captured.

Before year's end of 1992, Pichushkin claimed his first victim in curious fashion. First, he recruited classmate Mikhail Odiychuk to join him in a two-man team of killers, hunting in Bitsevski Park. Before departing on the hunt, Pichushkin sensed that Odiychuk was having second thoughts and teased him into writing a suicide note "as a joke." Once in the park, increasingly anxious, Odiychuk handed Pichushkin a length of rope he'd brought along, but Pichushkin whipped it around his friend's neck, strangling him and snapping his cervical vertebrae, then pushed his body down a manhole. Afterward, he burned his own clothes as a precaution and was ready with lies when Odiychuk's parents telephoned, seeking to learn their son's whereabouts, to which he pled ignorance. When the corpse turned up, police questioned him briefly, then accepted Odiychuk's note as genuine and closed the case as a suicide, but the near-miss chastened Alexander, prompting a nine-year moratorium on further homicides.

When he resumed killing in 2001, Pichushkin's prime targets were elderly men, often homeless, though he also found time to slay younger men, women, and children. In a typical attack, he would accost his prey at Bitsevski Park, offering vodka, then would strike his target from behind, crushing the victim's skull with a hammer or metal pipe and shoving a vodka bottle into the gaping wound. Attacks came from behind, he later told police, to keep blood off his clothes. As for his motive, he professed feeling like God, deciding who should live or die. "In all cases I killed for only one reason," he said. "I killed in order to live, because when you kill, you want to live. For me, life without murder is like life without food for you. I felt like the father of all these people, since it was me who opened the door for them to another world." Occasionally, Alexander skipped his vodka bottle "signature" and dropped unconscious prey into the sewer network underlying Bitsevski Park, trusting them to drown. That method also proved efficient for the most part, although one victim did manage to survive.

Moscow police had their hands full with murders in the 21st century. In July 2003, someone killed ten young women caught walking alone in various parts of the capital, strangling them or slashing their throats. Two more deaths in September prompted media speculation about a serial killer at large, but authorities — already conscious of the separate pattern of crimes around Bitsevski Park — tried to quash all such rumors. After the daily newspaper *Kommersant* ("The Businessman") speculated on *two* random killers at large in the city, a police spokesman sternly replied, "There is no maniac in Moscow."

Denials notwithstanding, officers *were* hunting the unknown "Bitsevski Park Maniac." In February 2006 they pursued an innocent suspect, shooting him in the leg, later exonerating him. Police also arrested a transvestite, found carrying a hammer in his purse at the park, but later released him without criminal charges.

While the murders of young women remained unsolved at last report, penned in 2007 by crime expert Katherine Ramsland, Sasha Pichushkin's luck ran out a year earlier, due to his own carelessness. His final victim was 36-year-old Marina Moskalyova, a coworker from the Moscow supermarket where Pichushkin's manager called him a "good natured" employee, adding that "when he came into contact with customers, he was polite and well mannered." Pichushkin invited Marina for a walk in the woods on June 5 and she agreed, leaving a note for her son that included Sasha's name and phone number. When her corpse was found in a babbling stream at Bitsevski Park, bearing the unknown slayer's trademark head wounds, police found security camera footage from a nearby railway platform, depicting Moskalyova strolling with Pichushkin hours before her murder. Police arrested him on June 16, at an apartment he shared with his mother. One piece of evidence collected from the flat was a hand-drawn chessboard with dates inscribed on 62 of its 64 squares.

Pichushkin initially denied any murders, then turned talkative and began leading police to sites where he had left his victims' bodies, reenacting many of the crimes on videotape. His favored spot for killing, Sasha claimed, was a place in Bitsevski Park where he once buried a pet dog — and that dog had special significance for one of the men he murdered. In 1996, he said, his pet had playfully sniffed at a dog owned by a neighbor, Valery Kulyazhov, who snapped at Pichushkin, "Take away that enormous mongrel mutt!" Nurturing that insult for a decade, Pichushkin had retaliated by killing Kulyazhov in 2006.

Considering his history and his admitted crimes, Pichushkin's sanity required evaluation prior to trial. Physicians at Serbsky State Scientific Center for Social and Forensic Psychiatry examined him for months on end, judging him sane and competent for trial, although they granted that he suffered from incurable antisocial personality disorder — also known as sociopathy or an impoverished moral sense or conscience disorder — and narcissistic personality disorder, a long-term pattern of abnormal behavior characterized by exaggerated feelings of self-importance, an excessive need for admiration, and a lack of understanding for others' feelings. Psychologist Mikhail Vinogradov blamed Sasha's crimes primarily on anger at his grandfather's "abandonment" in adolescence, but acknowledged "a sexual context," noting that Pichushkin described his killing spree as "a perpetual orgasm."

Pichushkin made his first court appearance on August 13, 2007, for a 15-minute preliminary hearing, confined — like his idol Chikatilo before him — inside a tempered glass cage to protect him from angry spectators. During those proceedings, he requested that his body count be raised to 60, from 49 as stated in his indictment, plus three counts of attempted murder for victims who survived their injuries. Prosecutor Yury Syomin successfully opposed that motion, telling the court, "There are no bodies, no fragments, not even records of people gone missing" to justify additional charges. Pichushkin also requested trial by jury, rather than a three-judge panel, a motion readily accepted by Judge Andrei Subarev, who scheduled Sasha's public trial to begin on September 13. Leaving court, when a reporter asked him why he'd killed, Pichushkin simply answered, "Such is the situation." Defense attorney Pavel Ivannikov was mum on the subject of a possible insanity plea, telling the press, "My client understands that he is to blame for most of these murders."

Pichushkin's trial opened on schedule, evidence unfolding while Sasha paced inside his glass cage. When the subject of his body count was raised, he rejected his goal of 64 victims, declaring, "I never would have stopped, never. They've saved many people by catching me." Indeed, he called himself a "hunter" and the "King of the Forest" while striking a philosopher's pose. Of his victims, Pichushkin said, "I liked to listen to their dreams, desires, and plans, because I already knew that none of them would ever come true."

One witness against him was Maria Viricheva, a young shop clerk from Tatarstan, whom he lured to the forest with an offer of black market goods, then pushed her down a 26-foot well. As Viricheva told the court, she "feverishly fumbled about in the walls of the tube and swam around in the muck for a whole hour" before securing handgrips and extricating herself. Psychologist Tatyana Drusinova testified that Pichushkin was "detached from human beings. Human beings were no more than wooden dolls, like chess pieces, to him," yet he was still legally sane. Sasha, for his part, described his first killing from 1992 as being "like first love — it's unforgettable." As for his final victim, Pichushkin claimed to know she'd left a note at home identifying him. "I burnt myself," he told the court, "so there's no need for the cops to take credit for catching me. I'm a professional."

Jurors convicted Pichushkin of 49 murders and three failed attempts on October 24, 2007. Judge Vladimir Usov used an hour of the court's time reading that verdict and naming the victims in order. Considering Russia's new moratorium on executions, Prosecutor Syomin requested a life prison term, and Judge Usov readily complied, adding a stipulation that Pichushkin should spend the first 15 years of his term in solitary confinement.

There he remains today, although his solitude was interrupted in March 2008 for an interview with journalist Yasha Levine from the tabloid *Tvoi Den* ("Your Day"). Pichushkin told Levine that he enjoyed taunting police, and that "riskier murders made him feel powerful, more powerful than the State." He raped no victims, but derived pleasure from "sexual substitution" — specifically "skeletal penetration, skullfucking." On entering prison, Pichushkin said, "I was not in a good mood. Now it's gotten better. I have completely adapted." Five-minute prison showers included "ideal water, so hot, I even have to dilute it with cold water," though he complained of receiving only one haircut so far. Recalling his baptism at age three, Pichushkin said, "I did not want it. I can also say that I will not either read the Bible or write an autobiography." Politically, he was meticulous: "As for voting, in all my 33 years, I have never missed a chance to vote." He reserved special scorn for his ex-defense attorney, telling Levine, "I would cut him open like a fish. I would have killed him like an insect, and I would receive much pleasure from the process. I would cut him up and make belts out of his flesh. But as for remembering everyone I killed, who and when and where, that, I don't remember. I don't even care to remember."

But others remembered and still searched for justice. One casualty of that search was Konstantin Kalashnikov, a policeman who took down the statement of a surviving victim in 2002, then refused to open an investigation of her case. Ex-officer Kalashnikov received a three-year prison sentence for his negligence, and his appeal was rejected on November 24, 2005.

14. Mikhail Popkov: "The Werewolf"

Serial killers often display a fascination for police work. Many follow investigations of their own crimes and may even inject themselves into the case, posing falsely as a witness or assisting in searches for missing victims. Others taunt authorities with letters, phone calls, and the like. Some attempt to become police officers, and having failed, settle for jobs in private security. A few actually make the cut to wear a badge that becomes their hunting license — but only one of those has managed to continue killing for nearly two decades.

Meet "The Werewolf," a demented lawman who allegedly set out to "cleanse the streets of prostitutes" in Angarsk, the administrative center of Angarsky District of Irkutsk Oblast, Russia, located on the Kitoy River.

Mikhail Viktorovich Popkov was born in Siberia on March 7, 1964. By his own later account, his mother — an abusive alcoholic — set him on the course that would consume his life and seal the fates of women whose appearance or behavior brought those ugly memories to mind. Final estimates of Popkov's body count, correlated with his escalating confessions, range from 22 to 82 victims.

After joining the Angarsk police department, Popkov met and married another officer, two years his junior, named Elena. Their only child, daughter Ekaterina or "Katya," was born in 1987, five years before Popkov reportedly claimed his first victim. Detectives, unaware that they were hunting one of their own, initially dubbed their unknown subject "The Wednesday Murderer" after the weekday when a number of his victims were discovered, left nude in woodlands or on roadsides. On several occasions, wife Elena furnished Popkov with an alibi for specific crime dates, which investigators failed to question. Even after he began confessing from a prison cell, authorities absolved Elena and Ekaterina of involvement in the crimes.

Popkov agreed that both women were innocent, telling authorities, "I had a double life. In one life I was an ordinary person. I was in the service in the police, having positive feedback on my work. I had a family. My wife and daughter considered me a good husband and father, which corresponded to reality. In my other life I committed murders, which I carefully concealed from everyone, realizing that this was a criminal offense. My wife and daughter never knew about the crimes I committed and did not even suspect this."

As for his choice of prey, Popkov portrayed it as random. "The victims were those who, unaccompanied by men, at night, without a certain purpose," he said, "were on the streets, behaving carelessly, who were not afraid to enter into conversation with me, get into my car, and then go for a drive in search of adventures, for the sake of entertainment, ready to drink alcohol and have sexual intercourse with me. They abandoned their husbands and went out to party as if it was the last day on Earth. Not all women became victims, but those of a certain negative behavior, I had a desire to teach and punish. Others did not behave in such a way, they were afraid. The exception was the murder of Elena Dorogova, who was hurrying to the [railway] station to meet her mother. On this occasion, the woman was sober." Investigators later noted that most of his victims were full-figured and of below average height—perhaps another echo of the mother Popkov despised.

Another victim who broke the usual pattern was a teacher at his daughter's music school. Popkov later said, "Her corpse was found in the forest along with the body of another woman. My daughter asked me to give her money, as the school was collecting to organize funerals, and I gave it to her."

In short, Popkov took victims as they came, often luring the tipsy ones for nighttime lifts home in his "safe" patrol car, then driving to remote locations, where he raped and murdered them. His first killing happened "spontaneously," Popkov said, adding, "I just felt I wanted to kill a woman I was giving a lift to in my car." Likewise, he claimed, "The choice of weapons for killing was always casual. I never prepared beforehand to commit a murder. I could use any object that was in the car — a knife, an axe, a bat. I never used rope for strangulation, and I did not have a firearm either." Some weapons, seized from criminals, he stole from the police station. "I had the opportunity then to take them," he explained. "Then I threw them away either at the crime scene or nearby, wiping them with something to remove my fingerprints."

Such a casual approach to murder sometimes breeds mistakes, of course. On one occasion, after assaulting two women together and leaving them for dead, Popkov realized that he had lost his police token — equivalent to a badge — during his struggle with the victims. Rushing back to the scene, Popkov said, "I found the token right away but saw that one of the women was still breathing. I was again shocked by the fact that she was still alive. I finished her with a shovel."

At least two other intended victims survived his attacks, and while one identified his picture from a police photo lineup, investigators chose to believe the alibi furnished by Popkov's wife. Elena and their daughter stood by Popkov after his arrest, apparently sincere in their conviction of his innocence. "We have been married for 28 years," Elena told reporters. "If I suspected something wrong, of course, I would divorce with him. I support him. I believe him. If he were to be released right now, I would not say a word and we would continue to live together."

Daughter Katya initially shared that opinion, saying, "I do not believe any of this. I always felt myself to be 'Daddy's girl.' For 25 years we were together, hand in hand. We walked, rode bikes, went to the shops, and he met me from school. We both collect model cars, so we have the same hobby. I wanted to be a criminologist, so I read a book with tips of how investigators catch serial killers and there were also basic classifications [of killers]. Daddy doesn't fit any of these classifications. He doesn't look like some maniac."

Later, as Popkov began to confess, both women — Katya now married, a teacher expecting a child of her own — left Angarsk to begin new lives in other cities, their illusions shattered.

Popkov rarely quibbled over details of his slayings, granting that he beheaded one woman, but staunchly denied removing another's heart, insisting, "I did not cut out the hearts of the victims." Or perhaps he just forgot, as numbers multiplied. He *did* admit, however, that he sometimes sampled necrophilia, raping his victims after death.

Another risk of raping strangers was disease. As Popkov told the tale, he stopped committing murders in 2000 after he contracted syphilis from one victim, whereupon he "became impotent." Around the same time, he left the police department to work as a security guard, first for Angarsk Oil and Chemical Company, and later for a private security agency.

By 2012, detectives realized they must consider the possibility of a killer cop at large. Some 3,500 past and present policemen — including Popkov — were asked to provide DNA samples, and all complied. Only Popkov's sample matched forensic evidence from multiple crime scenes, however, and officers arrested him on June 23, when he went to buy a new car in Vladivostok, the administrative center of Primorsky Krai, located around the Golden Horn Bay, near Russia's borders with China and North Korea. At the time, he was suspected of slaying 29 victims, ranging in age from 19 to 40 years old. After brief denials, Popkov confessed to those crimes and was formally charged on October 31 with 29 counts of murder, plus two attempted murders of surviving victims.

One living victim who agreed to testify at Popkov's trial was "Svetlana M.," attacked on January 29, 1998, when she was 15 "but looked older." She described how a policeman stopped to offer her a lift, then drove her to a forest near the village of Baikalsk, in the Slyudyansky District of Irkutsk Oblast, where he forced her to disrobe and bashed her head against a tree. She woke in a hospital bed the next day, having survived the night naked, in sub-freezing weather.

Despite her description of the officer, Elena Popkov gave her husband an alibi, and police spent years erroneously searching for a metalworker, professional driver, railway employee, heating station engineer, or a cemetery worker.

Even after Popkov's confession to 29 slayings, Nikolai Kitaev, an ex-police investigator critical of the manhunt's handling, suspected official files might contain "at least a dozen more" of Popkov's victims. In 2003, Mikhail Zavorin — a member of the original task force, said of Popkov, "He is charming and sociable. Women like him but he is a beast inside, and it is always hard to fight a werewolf."

At trial, in January 2015, Popkov told the Irkutsk Oblast Court, "I admit my guilt in full. Committing the murders, I was guided by my inner convictions." Russia's moratorium on capital punishment spared him, resulting in a life prison sentence, but prosecutors were not finished with him yet. By October of that same year, speculation flourished that he might have killed another 20 women scattered over Siberia and the Russian Far East, while some newspapers went further still, guessing at 61 murders in all. By March of 2017, Popkov himself had raised the total to 82 victims, still marveling at his ability to dupe police psychiatrists while he remained on active duty. "I never thought of myself as mentally unhealthy," he told the *Siberian Times.* "During my police service, I regularly passed medical commissions and was recognized as fit." Popkov called the tally of 82 murders his "final" figure — far eclipsing that of "Rostov Ripper" Andrei Chikatilo (Chapter 9), while still insisting that throughout the slayings "I was a good husband and father."

15. Sergei Martynov: "The Torso Killer"

Sergei Martynov presents a case study of what society may expect when it releases a serial killer from prison after his or her first homicide. The conundrum: if captured after a first offense and imprisoned, rather than being executed, no legal system on Earth permits officials to predict the future and anticipate more crimes as yet uncommitted.

Russia's future "Torso Killer" was born on June 2, 1962, at Nyazepetrovsk, the administrative center of Nyazepetrovsky District in Chelyabinsk Oblast, situated on the Nyazya River, 93 miles northwest of Chelyabinsk. He apparently avoided conflict with the law for 30 years before police arrested him for raping and killing an unidentified woman (or teenage girl, in some reports) and convicted him on those charges in 1992. Martynov served 13 years in custody, and like many convicts before him, he viewed prison more as a kind of "finishing school" than as a correctional institution. In fact, he was prepared to take up where he had left off, virtually from the moment of parole.

Soon after his release in 2005, Martynov attacked a young girl at knifepoint in Kemerovo, an industrial city and the administrative center of Kemerovo Oblast, in the Kuznetsk Basin of southwestern Siberia. He attempted to replicate his 1992 attack, but the victim survived and described him to police, who placed Martynov's name and photo on their "wanted" list.

Identification and capture were two very different things, however. In June 2007, Martynov murdered a woman in Glazov, a town in the Udmurt Republic, located on the Cheptsa River and beside the Trans-Siberian Railway. This time, he dismembered the corpse in a style that would earn him his "Torso Killer" nickname from the press. One month later, he raped an eight-year-old girl at Vyazovka, a village in Nizhny Novgorod Oblast, near the Volga River, but left his young victim alive. Ten months later, in May 2008, he killed a male victim during a robbery, then rebounded in June with an elderly woman slain and dismembered in rural woodlands. November 2008 saw another woman killed and mutilated in Oryol Oblast, located in the southwestern part of the Central Federal District, in the Central Russian Upland. In August 2010, the Torso Killer butchered 70-year-old Tamara Sadikova at Ufa, capital of the Republic of Bashkortostan, then resurfaced two months later to claim his final victim in Voronezh Oblast, occupying one-third of the whole area of Russia's Central Black Earth Region bordering Ukraine.

From the day of his parole, Martynov stayed ahead of manhunters by roaming over ten different oblasts of central and western Russia, but as his murder spree accelerated toward its climax, he began to taunt police with mocking notes left at crime scenes that officers described simply as "gruesome." One of three notes found with Tamara Sadikova in Ufa read simply: "You're rubbish. You'll never find me anyway!" Another, discovered in August 2010, invited police to meet Martynov at noon on a given day in Chelyabinsk, 130 miles south of Yekaterinburg, but when they rolled out in force, he was nowhere to be found.

Detectives finally staked their hopes on technology, tracing a cell phone Martynov stole from one of his victims, pouncing when he activated it on November 18, 2010. Surrounded, he offered no resistance and, in fact, told officers that he wanted to be captured. No further details of his crimes were publicized until May 23, 2012, when prosecutors listed a slate of charges against Martynov including "at least" eight murders, sexual assaults on two minor girls who survived after suffering grave injuries, assaults on many other victims, plus other counts of hooliganism and violent sexual actions. Police described Martynov as acting "daringly and cynically" during his five-year spree, afterward stating that his motive was an urge for "cleaning of the society." One victim, an eight-year-old girl, was the daughter of a man who hired Martynov to repair the family's roof in the Nizhny Novgorod Region. Despite repeated sexual assaults, investigators claimed, "He killed mainly not on sexual motives, but on personal dislike." Even in custody, he asked jailers to give him a cellmate whom he could murder "because he was bored."

With Martynov's trial looming in May 2012, the Russian public next heard from Vladimir Markin, a spokesman for *Sledstvennyi komitet* — the Investigative Committee of the Russian Federation — created in January 2011 to supplant the Russian Prosecutor General's Investigative Committee and operate as Russia's primary anti-corruption agency. He told reporters, "The investigators have established circumstances of eight murders committed by Martynov. An absolute majority of Martynov's victims were women, as well as two minor girls, against one of which Martynov had committed violent sexual actions and inflicted grave injuries to another. The investigators have collected enough evidence and the case is forwarded for the bill of particulars to be approved and then will be sent in to the court to be considered on merits."

And those particulars proved more than accurate. At trial in Voronezh Regional Court, Martynov was convicted on all counts filed against him and, in light of Russia's moratorium on executions, received a life prison term on November 10, 2012. Age 50 at the time of sentencing, the Torso Killer is not expected to emerge from prison a second time.

16. Alexander Tchayka: "The Fur Coats Hunter"

If America's Federal Bureau of Investigation excels at anything, above all else, it is at planting definitions of various crimes in the public mindset. Multiple murders, for instance, double and triple slayings, speak for themselves, while "mass murder" is defined as killing four or more victims at one location during one continuous event, whether it spans a few minutes or a period of days. "Spree killers" — also labeled "rampage killers" — murder two or more victims at more than one location, omitting an ill-defined "cooling-off period" between the slayings. Finally, serial killers were once defined by the FBI as those who kill three or more victims on separate occasions and at different locations, but that definition left out too many offenders who kill most victims at home (like Chicago's John Wayne Gacy) or in other close proximity to one another. The definition also failed to account for serial offenders caught or killed before claiming a third victim, which ultimately forced FBI headquarters to accept two or more victims, still slain with "cooling-off" gaps between crimes.

Depending on which definition one prefers, Alexander Nikolaevich Tchayka might be ranked either as a serial or spree killer, although occurrence of his homicides over a two-week period suggest the former may be more appropriate.

Tchayka was born on July 23, 1974, in Sumy, the administrative center of Sumy Raion (an administrative unit) of Sumy Oblast in the northwestern Ukrainian Soviet Socialist Republic. In

1984, at age 14, he was jailed for joining in the gang rape of a young girl, convicted and sentenced to five years at a penal colony near Kharkiv, the second-largest city in Ukraine and the largest in the administrative center of Kharkiv Oblast. Ideally, that sentence should have kept Tchayka off the streets until 1989, but in fact he was released on July 16, 1993, with a notation of "excellent behavior" rating early parole.

Once at liberty, Tchayka traveled from Ukraine to Moscow. There, the 19-year-old rapist killed his first victim on January 31, 1994, stabbing a 38-year-old woman 21 times and inflicting wounds so severe that her son could not identify the corpse. Like the rest of his victims, and many other women during Moscow's frigid winters, the target had been wearing a fur coat.

Only a week after his first slaying, on February 7, Tchayka struck again, this time stabbing a 50-year-old woman 17 times and stealing a gold ring from her hand. The next day, February 8, his 82-year-old third victim suffered eight stab wounds before losing a gold ring and her handbag. Finally, on February 12, Tchayka killed a 40-year-old woman. Witnesses to that attack described a tall young man dressed in a black coat and gray slacks, but the trail led no further.

Fearing more deaths to follow, police mounted an operation code-named *shuba* — "fur coat" — after the one thing all four Moscow victims had in common. Female officers dressed appropriately roamed the capital's streets, inviting attack, and while one of them was mugged at knifepoint, her assailant's weapon did not match the wounds inflicted on Tchayka's victims.

Then, on February 14, a plainclothes officer spotted a man matching the killer's description at the Frunzenskaya station on the Moscow Metro's Sokolnicheskaya Line. Deeming the young man's movements suspicious, the officer trailed him for several hours, then took Tchayka into custody for questioning. He cracked almost immediately, confessing all four homicides. Subsequently, at trial, he was convicted on all counts and sentenced to die, and while one published article claims that Tchayka was "executed sometime in the 1990s," all other reports agree that post-Communist Russia's moratorium on executions resulted in commutation of his sentence to life imprisonment. Spree killer or serial, the Fur Coats Hunter is now permanently out of circulation.

17. Vladimir Mukhankin: "The Pupil of Chikatilo"

Long after his execution, the shadow of serial killer Andrei Chikatilo (Chapter 9) still hangs over Rostov Oblast in Russia's Southern Federal District, where many of his victims were slain. Some killers who succeed him admit to patterning their crimes on Chikatilo's, or at least admiring him, but only one so far has dubbed himself "The Pupil of Chikatilo," operating in the same territory.

Vladimir Anatolyevich Mukhankin was born in the Zernogradsky District of Rostov Oblast, sprawling over 1,028 square miles of countryside, on April 22, 1960. His father, Mukhankin claims, abandoned his pregnant mother for another woman prior to Vladimir's birth, and his mother took her anger out on him with frequent beatings, allegedly after naming him in honor of Vladimir Lenin, the Soviet Union's founder. Away from his abusive home, Mukhankin faced more scorn and violence from schoolyard bullies, ending his formal education after only seven years. Later, as an adult, he married and fathered a son of his own, but tragedy struck again when the child drowned in the Kuban River, winding over 410 miles in the Northwest Caucasus region of European Russia.

It seems fair to say that Mukhankin's life was a lost cause thereafter, if not earlier. Whatever kinship he felt for Andrei Chikatilo consumed him, lapsing from admiration into emulation when Mukhankin reached age 35. During 1995 he committed nine murders and two attempted murders of women and girls, mostly in or around Shakhty, 47 miles northeast of Rostov-on-Don. Mukhankin typically stabbed or suffocated his victims, afterward dismembering and sometimes burning their corpses. He rarely committed rape, but did indulge in necrophilia with one 13-year-old victim, prompting police to speculate on his deep-seated hatred of females dating from childhood.

Mukhankin overreached his grisly game on May 1, 1995, when he attacked two victims — a mother and daughter — at once. He succeeded in killing the woman, but her child survived to identify their assailant. At Mukhankin's arrest, officers found a list of names identifying 40 policemen he hoped to murder, for reasons never clearly explained. In custody, he shed his early admiration of the Rostov Ripper, calling Chikatilo "a chicken" and faking erratic behavior in a bid to support an insanity defense at trial.

That effort failed, as a panel of psychiatrists labeled him legally sane. At trial, in January 1997, Mukhankin pled guilty on 22 felony counts, including eight murders, and the court sentenced him to death, but Russia's moratorium on capital punishment saw that sentence commuted to life imprisonment at Black Dolphin Prison in Sol-Iletsk, Orenburg Oblast, in the Ural Mountains.

At that, his commutation may have been no blessing for Mukhankin.

Formally named Penal Colony No. 6 of Russia's Federal Penitentiary Service, Black Dolphin Prison is renowned as one of the country's toughest lockups. Established in 1745 for inmates serving life terms at hard labor, it converted on November 1, 2000, to house only problem inmates sentenced to life. The prison's estimated 700 convicts include murderers, terrorists, cannibals, child molesters, and others simply tagged as "maniacs" but disqualified from more comfortable lodgings at an asylum. Guards blindfold inmates whenever they leave their cells, to prevent them studying the prison's layout for escape plans, and their vision is further stymied by walking hunched over, hands cuffed behind their backs and pulled upright by their uniformed escorts, a "stress position" designed for maximum physical control. Inmates spend all but 90 minutes of each day in solitary cells, transported to a cage for exercise during that hour and a half, while jailers search their cells for contraband. Between awakening each morning and lights-out at night, guards circulate at 15-minute intervals, ensuring that no inmate is caught lounging on his bunk. Four meals per day consist of soup alone, and prisoners must answer any order from a guard with "Yes, Citizen Chief" or face strict discipline.

Too harsh a home for the likes of Vladimir Mukhankin? Some human rights activists think so, with one — Pamela Engel — comparing conditions at Black Dolphin Prison to those found in "World War II concentration camps." Still, at last report, no formal inmate complaints had been filed — or, at least, none are acknowledged by prison administrators.

18. Tamara Samsonova: "Granny Ripper"

Casual observers of this killer's nickname might conclude that it refers to a male gerontophile offender with a penchant for mutilating elderly women, but they would be wrong. In fact, the slayer was herself a female pensioner, already old for a first-time serial killer when she began hunting senior citizens in 1995, claiming at least 13 lives over the next two decades.

Tamara Samsonova was born on February 5, 1947, in Saint Petersburg and spent her life there, in Russia's second-largest city. Though she clearly did not plan it at the time, a population of 5 million year-round residents by 2012, plus travelers arriving and departing on the Baltic Sea, made keeping track of everyone in town a virtual impossibility. As an adult, Tamara was confined to psychiatric hospitals on three separate occasions, resulting in diagnoses of possible schizophrenia: a mental disorder characterized by abnormal social behavior and failure to understand what is real, with symptoms including false beliefs, unclear or confused thinking, and claims of hearing disembodied voices. Nonetheless, she married and appeared to lead a fairly normal life — at least, until her husband disappeared without a trace in 2005. To this day, he has not been located, either alive or dead.

Police now think that Samsonova murdered him, but they possess no evidence. If true, he was a relatively late addition to her victims' list, and prosecutors do not need another corpse to keep Tamara out of circulation for the rest of her life.

Officers can only speculate as to how Samsonova concealed her crimes before she found herself suddenly single in 2005. She served as a paid caretaker for at least one victim — her last, a 79-year-old woman, Valentina Ulanova — whom she fed an overdose of sleeping pills on July 23, 2015, before dismembering her body with a hacksaw while Ulanova was still alive. Closed circuit television cameras caught Tamara on tape as she carried Valentina's truncated corpse in a black plastic bag and dumped it near a pond, where passers-by found one of the victim's arms and one leg three days later. Her motive for that slaying: a quarrel over unwashed plates and cups in Ulanova's sink.

Police arrested Samsonova on July 28, holding her for questioning on suspicion of committing a single murder. Searchers at her flat soon found the widow's diary, then recalled that a dismembered male victim was found on the same street, near the dumping pond, 12 years earlier.

As if that were not enough, Tamara's diary opened a grim new world for detectives, including 11 more slayings. One entry read: "I killed my tenant Volodya, cut him to pieces in the bathroom with a knife and put the pieces of his body in plastic bags and threw them away in the different parts of Frunzensky District" — a Saint Petersburg neighborhood of 14 square miles, with 401,779 inhabitants in 2010. While comparing diary entries to other unsolved cases of dismemberment, officers also had to wade through mundane comments inserted at random: "Slept badly...Drank coffee...Take medicines...I do not eat," and so on. One policeman who read the diary told reporters, "It was as if she was afraid to miss something important in her life."

By the time they'd read it all, officers suspected Samsonova of 13 murders besides Valentina Ulanova, and worse was yet to come. Soon, they began to speak of cannibalism. A spokesman for the Investigative Committee of the Russian Federation told journalists that various internal organs — and lungs in particular — had been excised from Samsonova's suspected victims. In a spirit of cooperation with her captors, she soon confessed to the other homicides.

At her first courtroom appearance, near July's end, Samsonova seemed less concerned with her pending charges than with reporters on hand and how they would describe her crimes. "I knew you would come," she told them in court. "It's such a disgrace for me, all the city will know." Judge Roman Chebotaryov brought her back on point, saying, "I am asked to arrest you. What do you think?" Samsonova replied, "You decide, Your Honor. After all, I am guilty and I deserve a punishment. I was getting ready for this court action for dozens of years. It was all done deliberately. There is no way to live. With this last murder I closed the chapter." After Chebotaryov remanded her into custody, Tamara clapped her hands as if in approval, then blew a kiss to reporters and said, "It's stuffy here. Can I go out?"

She could and did "go out" — to prison, where, at last report, she still awaited trial and sentencing. With executions held in abeyance throughout Russia, she would face a maximum term of life imprisonment, and how long could that be for a woman already 68 years old? One anonymous police investigator cautioned reporters, "She's either much more stupid, or much smarter, than she seems."

And she was correct about one thing, at least: her chapter was truly closed.

19. Maxim Petrov: "Doctor Death"

Worldwide, statistics indicate that roughly one in ten identified serial killers is associated in some way with the medical profession: doctors, nurses, nurses' aides, orderlies, even an occasional dentist. Some, like Britain's Dr. Harold Shipman, may kill hundreds of patients before they are unmasked as murderers. Others, like Dr. Joseph Michael Swango, traveled widely to avoid detection, claiming victims in several U.S. states before he moved on to different venues in Africa and Saudi Arabia. Despite the relative frequency of their appearance in headlines and on police blotters, each new example strikes the public as a shock, damaging trust in caretakers who literally hold our lives in their hands.

Maxim Vladimirovich Petrov is a native of St. Petersburg, born in 1965 when Russia's second-largest city still bore the Soviet name Leningrad, imposed in 1924 and only changed in 1991 by public referendum after Communism's downfall. More specifically, he lived and worked on the central city's Vasilyevsky Island, bounded by the Bolshaya Neva and Malaya Neva Rivers to the south and northeast, and by the Gulf of Finland to the west. Twice married and the father of three children, he spent his working hours in a hospital emergency room, deciding at age 32 to expand his venue, adding house calls to the list and turning patients into prey.

Dr. Petrov began his career in crime as a thief, in 1997, surprising elderly patients with unscheduled visits at their homes, usually during morning hours when other family members were at work. After checking each patient's blood pressure, he expressed alarm and suggested a sedative injection to "relax" them. While they were unconscious, Petrov prowled their homes, stealing any valuables he could carry away, even filching rings and other jewelry from his victims while they lay drugged.

Petrov's early guinea pigs were lucky; they survived and woke after he left their homes, seemingly unaware that they'd been robbed while in drug-addled states. In all, he would confess to 47 robberies at his arrest, three years after the thefts began, 29 committed before the first victim died on February 2, 1999. On that occasion, he was startled by a patient's daughter while he robbed their house and panicked, stabbing the younger woman with a handy screwdriver, then strangling her unconscious mother with a nylon stocking. After that experience, he changed his *modus operandi* to include a lethal mix of drugs, inducing death while, as he hoped, persuading homicide investigators that the killer had no real medical knowledge. That done, he would proceed to rob each house in turn, then set the homes on fire in a bid to destroy forensic evidence.

So he went on through 1999 and into 2000, while police cast about in vain for a suspect. Finally, hoping for clues, detectives learned almost by accident how Petrov chose his victims. All were on a local health center's list of pulmonary patients who had undergone photofluorography, a type of chest X-ray screening used to diagnose lung cancer or tuberculosis. From that beginning, investigators launched Operation *Medbrat* ("male nurse"), involving 700 officers. They soon compiled another list, this one including 72 X-ray subjects earmarked as possible victims of future attacks.

Dr. Petrov sprang the trap on January 17, 2000, when he paid his latest unannounced house call on one of the listed potential victims. Placed under arrest, he first admitted killing 19 persons, then recanted that statement, blaming his admission on "intense psychological pressure" he suffered while in custody. By then, it scarcely mattered, though. A search of his apartment turned up items stolen from some of the many victims, and police traced other pieces to the market where he'd sold them off for cash.

At trial in December 2002, that evidence was used against him, as was testimony from five intended victims who survived, though some were seriously injured. Anastasia Plotnikova told the court, "I remember a call at my flat at about 2:00 p.m. The young man presented himself as a doctor from the local clinic. The doctor took my blood pressure, which appeared to be high, and offered an injection. He spent a lot of time trying to find the vein, and I thought, 'How can a doctor have problems with such a thing?' When I woke, there was fire around me. I cried for help on the balcony. The fire service came but the flat was badly burned." When the smoke cleared, Ms. Plotnikova missed her wedding rings, a pair of gold earrings, and — almost bizarrely — two packets of tea.

Another victim, Valentina Pleshikova, said that she was only saved because her husband had returned early from work. She told the court how Petrov had injected her with unknown drugs, waking later to find her gas oven turned on with the pilot light off and the home's windows shut. After her husband rescued her and cleared the house of gas, they found a set of silver forks and 200 rubles (about $3.44 in U.S. dollars) missing, along with some coffee.

Petrov, dubbed "Doctor Death" and "Doctor Killer" by the media, insisted he was innocent, penning a letter from his cell to the National Media Group's Channel Five in St. Petersburg, denouncing their series of reports on his case as "libelous." At the same time, reporters cast Petrov as a cold-blooded killer who enjoyed his moment in the glaring lights of fame.

At the conclusion of Petrov's trial in late November 2002, Judge Valentina Kudriashovo declared, "Five victims have spoken. They are all very old people. This will not be a quick process. He is accused of a series of robberies and killings." Still, she had no problem convicting Petrov in the first week of December, finding him guilty of 12 murders — seven other homicide counts had been dropped for insufficient evidence — plus various lesser felonies. In the absence of a functional Russian death penalty, Maxim Petrov received a sentence of life imprisonment.

20. Viktor Sotnikov

Serial killers are remembered on the basis of their notoriety, specifically their body counts or other features of their case that capture the public's imagination. Viktor Viktorovich Sotnikov is a rare example of a murderer who had so little impact on Russian society, despite his record of claiming eight victims, that reporters never even bothered to tag him with a catchy nickname.

Part of Sotnikov's publicity problem was chronological, part geographical, another part demographic. His homicides spanned 12 years, between 2000 and 2011, giving citizens time to forget some of his crimes, and he did all his hunting in neighboring Lipetsk Oblast and Tambov Oblast, both located in Russia's Central Black Earth economic region, with Tambov Oblast primarily comprising forest steppes. The two oblasts rank near the low end in population density among Russia's 46 oblasts (or federal subjects). Between them, they claimed a total population of 2,265,507 inhabitants in 2010, from Russia's total population of 144 million.

On top of all that, Viktor Sotnikov was another late-blooming serial killer. Born in 1961 at Gryazi, the administrative center of Gryazinsky District in Lipetsk Oblast, but he did not start killing until age 39, while most serial slayers begin in their early twenties or even younger. Even then, he required an accomplice for several murders, further diluting his potential notoriety. Finally, he left two of his victims to freeze in winter weather, leaving their deaths open to interpretation as accidental.

Indeed, if reporters had bothered to tag Sotnikov, they might well have called him "The Haphazard Killer."

As a youth, raised in an unstable household, Sotnikov began torturing animals and, on one occasion, hanged his own family's dog. Later, as he grew taller and stronger, he physically abused his parents and sisters, while selling bootleg liquor to earn pocket money. During that same period, he allegedly raped two women, then paid them from his moonshine fund to drop their accusations against him.

Sotnikov killed first on September 30, 2000, when he allegedly picked up a 19-year-old hitchhiker and persuaded her to stop by his house for a sociable drink. There, he said, they argued and he wound up beating her to death. The victim's mother, though not present, denied that version of events, insisting that he dragged her daughter forcibly into his home. In either case, the result was the same.

Viktor waited two years to select his next victim, while riding with companion Alexander Lenshin. They spied another hitchhiker, this one a 25-year-old woman, and offered her a lift, which she accepted. Inside the car, the woman resisted their sexual advances, whereupon Sotnikov beat her in a frenzied rage and Lenshin stabbed her in the chest. Afterward, they tried to dump her body into the Matyra River, which flows through both Tambov and Lipetsk Oblasts, but could not prevent the corpse from surfacing. Frustrated, they eventually hid her remains in rubble at an abandoned limestone crushing plant.

On January 1, 2003, Sotnikov and Lenshin found a 31-year-old woman intoxicated and walking on her own, after a New Year's party. They dragged her into their car and drove to a deserted area of Lipetsk Oblast, then tossed her from the vehicle alive, leaving her to freeze overnight in the sub-zero weather.

March of 2003 found Sotnikov and Lenshin back on the prowl, this time in the agricultural Petrovsky District of Tambov Oblast. This time, the hitchhiker they chose was a 46-year-old man en route to Tambov, but he never made it. The killers bludgeoned him and dumped him at roadside, covering his corpse with snow. A few days later, they murdered another man — a 66-year-old pensioner — who asked them for a lift to the Dobrinsky District of Lipetsk Oblast.

In December 2005, Viktor was back to the hunt on his own, promising a 32-year-old woman a lift to Lipetsk if she would share drinks with him first. That done, he drove his tipsy passenger instead to Matyrskomu Reservoir, shoving her out of his car and leaving her to die from hypothermia overnight.

Sotnikov then took another hiatus — four years and four months in duration this time — before making his next foray in April 2010, accompanied on that occasion by his wife. She looked on, apparently without objections, while he picked up another hitchhiking girl and drove to the Matyra River, there slaying his captive and setting her body on fire.

Another nineteen months elapsed before Viktor's last murder, in November 2011. Selecting a homeless man as the victim, he asked his target to help him collect firewood, then killed him in the forest and left the body there. Alas, multiple witnesses came forward who had seen him with the victim and who told their stories to police. Arrested on the basis of their revelations, Sotnikov tried to plead insanity, but forensic psychiatrists refuted that ruse. In October 2013, a court judged him guilty on eight counts of murder and imposed a life prison term. Accomplice Alexander Lenshin, also in the dock, received a 19-year sentence as an accomplice to four of the murders.

21. Irina Gaidamachuk: "Satan in a Skirt"

Irina Viktorovna Gaidamachuk took her vodka seriously. Many Russians do, of course, but she took it *so* seriously that when cash ran short, she turned to homicide for extra money, killing even when she lost count of her victims after slaying 10.

Russia's future "Satan in a Skirt" was born in 1972 at Nyagan, a town in the northwest of Khanty-Mansi Autonomous Okrug, located near the Ob River and 140 miles northwest of Khanty-Mansiysk, an oil boom town and the administrative center of the autonomous district. She drank heavily from childhood, prompting state authorities to remove her from her negligent parents' custody, but the change did Irina no good. As an adult, she moved to Krasnoufimsk, a town on the Ufa River in Sverdlovsk Oblast, in the Ural Federal District. There, she met and married husband Yury and bore him two children before her drinking lapsed out of control. At length, in 2002, Yury refused to give her any household money, fearing she would waste it all on vodka while their children were neglected.

Refusing to abandon her one and only hobby, Irina hit upon a grim solution. Posing as a social worker, she gained access to the homes of older women, whom she murdered by strangulation or with an axe or hammer, afterward stealing whatever money she could find. After some homicides, Irina torched their homes in an effort to cover her tracks, sometimes sober enough to make the fires seem accidental. Although her liquor-addled brain lost count, she claimed 17 victims over eight years' time, most of the crimes logged in Krasnoufimsk, though some also occurred in other towns scattered around Sverdlovsk Oblast, including Achit, Druzhinino, Serov, and Yekaterinburg.

Despite her efforts to stage accidents, police were on the case, but Irina's method of dispatching those she killed convinced detectives that the slayer must be male. Grilling some 3,000 suspects in all, they even speculated that they might be looking for a man in drag, donning women's clothes to deceive his intended victims. After all, what woman would attack another female in such brutal fashion, throttling or beating her to death? With men, however — "maniacs" in Russian parlance — hacking, clubbing wounds were almost *de rigueur*.

At last, Irina's drunken clumsiness betrayed her. In 2010 she attacked an elderly woman who managed to escape and tell police that her assailant was female. Officers initially jailed an innocent woman, 29-year-old Irina Valeyeva, coercing her into a full confession, but Gaidamachuk blundered on in her mindless pursuit of alcohol. Soon afterward, she struck again, and while Irina successfully killed final victim Alexandra Povaritsyna — after changing her *modus operandi*, dropping the social worker façade and offering to redecorate Povaritsyna's apartment — one of the dead woman's neighbors saw her leaving the crime scene, furnishing police with a clear description. Arrested at last, she confessed her crimes and told jailers, "I just wanted to be a normal mother but I had a craving for drink. My husband Yury wouldn't give me money for vodka."

Husband Yury, meanwhile, proclaimed himself clueless. Already squiring a new woman while his wife sat in jail, he told reporters, "I lived with her for 14 years but never suspected anything."

As in other cases, authorities sought to determine their suspect's sanity, submitting her to examination by experts from Moscow's Serbsky State Scientific Center for Social and Forensic Psychiatry. The doctors determined that, while Irina displayed "some mental illness," she was legally sane during her crime spree. Hearing that, Irina recanted her jailhouse confessions, but it did no good. Her trial began at Yekaterinburg in February 2012 and ended in June with conviction on all counts: 17 murder charges for victims aged from 61 to 89, plus one count of attempted murder. All told, she stole roughly 78,000 rubles — about $1,349 — from the 17 victims she killed.

Perhaps because she was a member of the "gentle sex," the court sentenced Irina to 20 years in prison — a term, outraged survivors of her victims noted, which amounted to just over one year per murder. They demanded life imprisonment but could not change the judge's mind. If Irina survives in prison, she should be back on the street — and back in the bars — sometime during 2032, at age 60. Defense attorney Suren Sarkisya claims even a 20-year term is excessive for Irina, announcing plans for ongoing appeals.

22. The Ryno-Skachevsky Gang

With Hitler's 1941 invasion of the Soviet Union, most Russians united in the crusade against Fascism. Small pockets of far-right sympathy remained — some exiled to China, like the Russian Fascist Organization, and several variations on the Hitler Youth — but Stalin's secret police soon liquidated or imprisoned those would-be Nazis remaining in the USSR. For decades after World War II, expression of such sentiments was banned by law, but Communism's collapse in 1991 opened a whole new world for the racist, ultra-nationalist right.

First to appear, in 1992, was the Russian National Socialist Party. Others soon followed, including Russian National Unity, the Russian National Union, the Slavic Union, the Autonomous Combat Terrorist Organization, and others. Wherever neo-Nazism reared its ugly head, young men and women — self-styled racist "skinheads" — were the fighting shockwave. Between 2004 and 2009, such hooligans murdered more than 550 victims across Russia, their targets including Jews, Muslims, and any immigrants viewed as "non-Slavic." Russia's Federal Security Service, successor to the KGB, estimated skinhead numbers between 2,000 and 3,000 in February 2009, with recruiting on the rise and no one entirely safe from their mayhem.

One teenage group that claimed a ghastly score, reportedly attacking 37 immigrants from the Caucasus and Middle Asia between August 2006 and October 2007, was the "Ryno-Skachevsky Gang," founded by cohorts Artur Ryno and Pavel Skachevsky, both born in 1988 and members of the Slavic Union when they met in Moscow, gathering other like-minded bigots to their cause. In the wake of their arrests, Slavic Union leader Dmitry Demushkin quickly distanced himself and his 1,500 followers from the savage skins, saying of Ryno and Skachevsky, "I didn't know them personally. They were young guys sitting in the corner of the meetings. They were quiet, mouse-like." Of course, Demushkin also disavowed a fellow Slavic Union leader, Nikola Korolev, jailed in August 2006 for bombing a Vietnamese café at Moscow's Cherkizovsky Market, killing 14 persons and wounding 49. "These tactics," Demushkin proclaimed, "were wrong."

Artur Ryno was born and raised in the southern Urals city of Yekaterinburg, where his parents soon divorced. Ironically, his father — from Russia's Far Eastern province of Chukotka — might himself have been a target for the future gang's attack, based on his non-Slavic features, passed down to Artur. Quiet and introverted at school, Ryno showed an aptitude for drawing and was enrolled at the Moscow School of Painting, Sculpture and Architecture when arrested, studying to paint classic Russian icons. His lawyers claim he turned to racism after a Chechen classmate beat him up at school. Moving to Moscow in 2006, Ryno shaved his head and met Pavel Skachevsky through an ultra-nationalist Internet website.

Skachevsky, born in Moscow, is the son of a deputy school headmistress and a "gifted" student who blames his descent into Fascism on the loss of a friend, killed when Chechen separatists bombed a series of apartment houses in September 1999, killing 293 persons and injuring more than 1,000. When arrested, Pavel was a student at Moscow's Russian State University of Physical Education, Sport, Youth, and Tourism.

Together, the pair gathered roughly a dozen like-minded skinheads, described by one reporter as "a geeky-looking bunch." The tallest of the lot was 22-year-old Svetlana Avvakumova, who videotaped the gang's attack on a Chinese youth, prompting her arrest in February 2008. Despite Avvakumova's racist views and savage actions, her mother claims, "Svetlana was always an innocent. As a girl she was a bit of a tomboy. She liked football and used to watch Spartak Moscow FC [Football Club]." Yelena Avvakumova marveled at her daughter's downfall, telling reporters, "My father was a tank commander during the war. He was severely injured during the battle for Königsberg; it left him disabled. He personally fought Fascism. Svetlana understands perfectly what Fascism is. We still have her grandfather's medals."

Clearly, though, the gap between understanding and avoidance is a yawning void.

It is a testament to Russia's plague of racist violence that Moscow police were ignorant of the Ryno-Skachevsky Gang's existence until April 16, 2007, when its members set upon Karen Abramian, the 46-year-old Armenian boss of a Moscow insurance company, outside his home. Abramian offered money and begged for his life, but Ryno and Skachevsky ignored his pleas, stabbing him 56 times. Before dying, Abramian identified his assailants simply as "skinheads." He'd also grabbed one of his killers by the arm, leaving a bloody print, and officers captured both youths on a streetcar leaving the crime scene, one still carrying a bloodstained knife, after Abramian's neighbors pursued them. Footage from security cameras also confirmed their role in the attack.

In custody, far from denying their guilt, Ryno and Skachevsky freely admitted assaulting at least 32 victims — 20 of whom they had murdered — over the past nine months. Moscow authorities initially dismissed that claim as youthful boasting, but perusal of their unsolved files produced more victims' names. Another stabbing murder, of Tajik immigrant Kyril Sadikov, occurred only three hours before the Abramian attack. Afterward, Ryno and Skachevsky enjoyed a meal, then set out in search of more prey.

Still, the "racially superior" skinheads were not infallible. Sometimes they judged victims by skin pigmentation alone and wound up killing or wounding actual ethnic Russians. One such mistake involved Uzbek student S. Azimov, ambushed outside his apartment on Zoe and Alexander Kosmodimiyansky Street, in Moscow's northwest suburb of Voikovskaya. Ryno and Skachevsky stabbed Azimov 56 times, then severed one ear as an afterthought while he lay dying. Such overkill was typical of the gang's assaults, often carried out near suburban metro stations, with victims stabbed between 15 and 60 times. Nor did Ryno and Skachevsky lack competition. According to Moscow's SOVA Center for Information and Analysis, which tracks hate crimes, racists murdered 50 victims in 2004, 47 in 2005, 64 in 2006, and 86 in 2007. In 2008, while Ryno and Skachevsky sat in jail, their ideological comrades murdered 96 persons and injured another 419.

In his first statement, Artur Ryno told police the gang's attacks began on August 21, 2007, the same day Slavic Union member Nikola Korolev bombed the Cherkizovsky Market, owned by immigrants from the Caucasus and Central Asia. In May of 2007, he raised no objection to journalists boosting his claims from 37 attacks to 37 murders, but that changed on June 13 when Ryno recanted his original confession. Pavel Skachevsky, for his part, staunchly denied participating in any homicides. Waffling statements aside, a 45-page indictment named both skinheads as participants in multiple attacks. Aside from Karen Abramian, specified victims included Sergei Nikolayev, a renowned chess player from Russia's Republic of Yakutia, fatally stabbed on October 20, 2007, and an Uzbek street cleaner, Rustam Gulimov, who survived his severe injuries. Altogether, open police files listed 27 racist attacks across Moscow on the same day Sergei Nikolayev was slain.

In addition to Ryno and Skachevsky, police jailed six of their followers, ranging in age from 14 to 18 years. One of those seized, "tomboy" Svetlana Avvakumova, had videotaped some assaults and uploaded them onto the Internet as inspiration for other skinheads. Others detained included 16-year-old Nikolai Dagaev, 18-year-old Denis Lavrenenkov, and 19-year-old Ivan Kitaikin. Lavrenenkov had also been detained in late 2006 for detonating a homemade bomb at the home of an anti-Fascist activist, but was released for lack of evidence. By July 1, 2008, all faced charges under various articles of the Russian Criminal Code, including incitement of hatred and hostility perfected with use of violence by an organized group; the attempted murder of two or more people by an organized group, through a hooligan impulse, and based on racial hatred and hostility; premeditated hooliganism by an organized group; and premeditated robbery by an organized group.

At the conclusion of the gang's mass trial, on December 15, 2008, a Moscow court found seven gang members guilty of 20 racist murders and 12 attempted murders. Ringleaders Ryno and Skachevsky, both legal minors when their crimes occurred, received the maximum permissible sentence of 10 years confinement at a medium-security prison. They were also ordered to pay two surviving victims compensation in the amount of 8,277,120 rubles ($144,000). The stiffest sentence fell to 20-year-old Roman Kuzin, who was jailed for 20 years. Another, Vitaly Nikitin, received a 12-year prison term. Four other defendants received six-year sentences, while two were acquitted on grounds of insufficient evidence.

Finally, in May 2009, the British Home Office added Artur Ryno and Pavel Skachevsky to a list of individuals banned from entering the United Kingdom as "leaders of a violent gang that beat migrants and posted films of their attacks on the Internet. Considered to be engaging in unacceptable behavior by fomenting serious criminal activity and seeking to provoke others to serious criminal acts." It hardly mattered at the time, since neither skinhead thug would be at liberty to travel anywhere before the year 2018.

23. "The Amazon Gang"

Team serial killers come in all permutations; parent and child, siblings or cousins, married couples or lovers, friends, even devotees to the same religion or political ideology. Rarest of all is an extended family that kills together for "sport" or profit, and Russia's most notorious family is "The Amazon Gang," so called because its members included a wife and mother — also dubbed "Russia's Ma Barker" after a reputed outlaw leader from the United States in the 1930s — plus her two daughters and the confessed ringleader's second husband.

The brains and driving force behind the gang was Inessa Tarverdiyeva, an ex-kindergarten teacher and self-proclaimed "gangster by nature," born in 1967. The group's other "Amazons" were daughters Viktoria, born in 1988, and Anastasiya, born in 1999. Rounding off the group, and its only male member, was Inessa's second husband (and Anastasiya's father), dentist Roman Podkopaev, born in 1978.

While some published reports credit the gang with crimes dating from 1998, a year before Anastasiya's birth, police officially list incidents occurring between 2007 and 2013, including the murders of "at least 30 people including women and children." Robbery was their prevailing motivation, prompting them to travel miles from their comfortable home in Stavropol, administrative center of Stavropol Krai, in the North Caucasus region in Southern Russia, seeking prey to rob and kill. Aside from random targets of opportunity, Inessa Tarverdiyeva loathed policemen, adding six officers to her family's list of victims, afterward robbing them of weapons and cash. Despite Anastasiya's youth when the murders began, police in Rostov Oblast say that all five members of the clan "actively took part in all crimes." Kingpin Inessa agreed, saying that homicide and robbery were like "going to the office for a day's work." Violent crime, to her brood, was simply an easier "means of earning money."

Neighbors in Stavropol suspected nothing amiss, since the Amazon Gang disguised their bloody forays as family camping trips. Vladimir Markin, heading the Investigative Committee of the Russian Federation, told journalists in 2013, "They looked like a totally good, nice family. Imagine them — a mother, a father, two children, including an underage girl. I am sure that when they were together, one could hardly imagine that they could even plan a crime."

Then again, Markin also told reporters, around the same time, that he was certain American astronauts had never walked on the moon during any of their highly publicized missions between 1969 and 1972.

One of the family's most vicious murders occurred in 2009, when they waylaid paratrooper Dmitry Chudakov, his wife Irina, and their two children at a highway rest stop. Point-blank fire from a semiautomatic weapon killed Dmitry, Irene, and seven-year-old son Sasha, while 11-year-old daughter Veronika suffered 37 stab wounds. Afterward the gang stole a laptop computer, hair dryer and camera, valued altogether at 73,689 rubles ($1,280). Perhaps realizing that even she must draw the line somewhere, Inessa later told police, "It was not me who killed the children. My husband shot them." Of course, Veronika

Chudakov was not shot — and by the time Inessa issued her disclaimer, Roman Podkopaev was dead, unable to speak for himself.

Another of the gang's raids claimed the life of Inessa's goddaughter. They targeted her home because the girl's father was an avid hunter, keeping a stockpile of rifles and shotguns. Tarverdiyeva's brood broke into the house and waited for the girl's parents to return, but were surprised when the goddaughter and a female friend arrived instead. Passing the time, the home invaders tortured and murdered both girls, gouging out their eyes.

The end came on September 8, 2013, when Inessa's family sought to rob a former military officer residing with his wife on Baklanova Street in Aksay, the administrative center of Aksaysky District in Rostov Oblast, located on the right bank of the Don River, 11 miles northeast of Rostov-on-Don. After murdering the couple, they searched the house but found no cash, settling for a meager haul of liquor, candles, and chicken drumsticks from the victims' refrigerator. Roman Podkopaev and adopted daughter Viktoria tried to flee the scene on a scooter, but were halted minutes later at a police checkpoint. When asked for his identification, Podkopaev drew a pistol instead, slaying Officer Ivan Shakhovoi. Wounded by the same burst of shots, Officer Aleksey Lagoda returned fire, killing Podkopaev and seriously wounding Viktoria.

From there, it was a relatively short step to a campsite where police found Inessa and daughter Anastasiya with an arsenal of 20 weapons, including automatic rifles, shotguns, firearms silencers, ammunition, and hand grenades. Officers also seized walkie-talkie radios, used by the gang to coordinate their movements and keep track of police responses. Detectives subsequently arrested Podkopaev's sister, 31-year-old Anastasia Sinelnik, and her husband—a 31-year-old former traffic patrolman—on suspicion of aiding and abetting the crime family by identifying robbery targets and concealing stolen loot. Weeping in court, Anastasia denied any complicity but refused to say if she had knowledge of her family's crime spree. Unnamed investigators say that Anastasia's husband played no part in the murders but willingly hid stolen items at his home, while Anastasia took stolen jewelry out for sale or to be remodeled as new items.

Research into Tarverdiyeva's background left several mysteries unresolved. While she admitted killing policemen, she refused to explain why she hated them. One theory, unsubstantiated, claimed that an officer she loved years earlier had left her for another woman. A friend of Tarverdiyeva filled in some blanks, saying, "She grew up with her mother, stepfather and younger brother. The family was a good one. Inessa was a beauty and many young men liked her, but her stepfather watched that she was back home in time and she argued with him about it. She fell in love with an Azerbaijani man called Arzu, Viktoria's father. He died in mysterious circumstances at a power station where he worked." The friend added that family acquaintances suspected Roman Podkopaev of killing Arzu, but he was never charged and later married Inessa himself. "Inessa's younger brother openly talked about it," the friend related. "I rarely met Inessa afterwards, and only know that she had one more daughter later."

Charges ultimately filed against Inessa and her daughters include the following crimes:

February 17, 2008 — the murder in Aksay of Zlydneva Michael, chief of the information security department of the Federal Drug Control, and his wife in their home before the killers stole coats, a jacket, and a television tuner.

July 17, 2008 — a highway shooting near Aksay that killed Rostov Alexey Sazonov and wounded female companion Yulia Vasilyeva, after which the killers stole Yulia's purse, driver's license, and passport.

March 10, 2009 — a home invasion on the outskirts of Novocherkassk in Rostov Oblast, where two residents were shot with a Saiga semi-automatic rifle, then finished off with knives. Stolen from the home were passports, a laptop, a camera and camcorder, plus women's boots, coats and men's jackets.

July 8, 2009 — the aforementioned Chudakov family massacre near Aksay, Rostov Oblast.

September 19, 2012 — two private security guards slain in Novocherkassk as they answered a dental clinic's burglar alarm. The killers used three stolen police weapons, including a submachine gun and two pistols, afterward stealing guns from both victims.

November 29, 2012 — a home invasion robbery at Novocherkassk. When the home owner gave chase, the bandits killed him with a pistol taken from one of their September 19th victims.

March 16, 2013 — Aksay traffic inspector Nikolai Kutsekon shot and killed when he responded to a car alarm sounding near his home and attempted to detain the would-be thieves.

April 8, 2013 — two victims shot, Yuri Statsenko fatally, on the outskirts of Novocherkassk, when they left their auto shop to investigate a burglar alarm. Again, the killers used a weapon stolen from their prior victims on September 19, 2012.

April 24, 2013 — an attempted home invasion in the Aksay district, where traffic inspector Andrew Jurin pursued the family's car and suffered fatal gunshot wounds. Inessa's tribe returned to the same house later, but the tenants foiled them with locked doors.

September 8, 2013 — the gang's last stand, described above, resulting in the death of one policeman and Inessa Tarverdiyeva's husband.

Despite the list of charges filed, accompanied by Inessa's confessions and recreation of the crimes using harmless model guns to demonstrate her murder technique, the Amazon Gang's surviving members had yet to face trial as *Iron Curtain Killers* went to press. Their most recent hearing convened at Rostov-on-Don Regional court, on January 12, 2017, with no further proceedings reported to date.

24. Alexander Bychkov: "The Belinsky Cannibal"

At least at first glance, Russia seems to have more than its share of cannibal killers. Expressed motives vary widely from one case to another, but the offender known as "The Belinsky Cannibal" may be the only such offender on record to claim that he killed and devoured strangers in a bid to impress his girlfriend.

Alexander Vladimirovich Bychkov was born to parents Vladimir and Irina on April 1, 1988, in Belinsky, the administrative center of Belinsky District in Penza Oblast, located at the confluence of the Bolshoy and Maly Chembar Rivers, some 300 miles southeast of Moscow. Unlike other slayers, who wander widely and compulsively, it appears that Bychkov never strayed more than a stone's throw from his hometown.

Bychkov's family occupied a home owned by his maternal grandmother, adding a fourth member with the birth of younger son Sergei in 1990. Both parents were alcoholics, father Vladimir working whatever odd jobs he could handle while Irina forced her sons to labor long hours at home. If not tilling the family's vegetable garden, Alexander and Sergei were sent to collect scrap metal for sale and work for neighbors, suffering beatings if they returned home empty-handed. In self-defense, the brothers turned to petty theft and, although caught at it several times, they escaped legal punishment when their shopkeeper victims took pity on their wretched situation. Vladimir Bychkov hanged himself at age 40, with neighbors blaming the combination of vodka and his wife's flagrant infidelity.

Alexander tried college in the 21st century, but dropped out to care for his brother after Sergei was severely beaten and thrown from a moving car, suffering a brain injury that left him partially disabled. Interfamilial tension only increased thereafter, made worse still when Alexander finally left home in 2009 to live with a girlfriend. That relationship ended when the girl ordered him out, branding him a "wimp" unworthy of her time. Above all else, that insult stung. As Bychkov later sketched his motive for police: "She said I was a wimp, not a wolf. I will show her. Maybe she will stop complaining and understand that I am a lone wolf."

For starters, he began to call himself "Rambo" after the movie tough guy portrayed by actor Sylvester Stallone in the Hollywood films *First Blood* (1982) and its three sequels. Sadly, for Bychkov and his future victims, self-imposed nicknames rarely constitute a personality makeover. He knew he would have to try harder — and why not by killing homeless alcoholic men who reminded him of his hated father?

On September 17, 2009, Bychkov met 60-year-old Yevgeni Zhidkov at a local tavern. Zhidkov was in Belinsky to complete paperwork allowing disbursement of his pension from a far-off government archive, and he gladly accepted Bychkov's offer of a free room for the night. Once they arrived and Zhidkov fell asleep, Alexander stabbed him to death, then dismembered his corpse.

Over the next three years, Bychkov repeated the pattern of his first murder, targeting homeless alcoholics, luring them to his house or to some other isolated spot before he killed them with hammer or a large knife resembling one carried by Stallone in his "Rambo" films. Afterward, he severed their heads and limbs, then buried the remains in his own backyard or at Belinsky's garbage dump. A calculating killer, Alexander usually struck in spring or summer, hoping that police would place the blame on migrant workers if his victims were discovered. One man who broke that pattern was an acquaintance who suspected Bychkov of murder and made the mistake of trying to blackmail him.

Belinsky police discovered their first identified Bychkov victim — Sergei Berezovsky, an ex-lover of Alexander's mother — in spring of 2010. September of that year revealed two more dismembered corpses, whereupon detectives arrested a mentally ill suspect, Alexander Zhuplov (or "Guplov" in one report), on September 19. In his addled state, assisted by police coercion, Zhuplov confessed to all three murders at a whirlwind trial and was consigned to a mental institution, while Bychkov continued his rampage.

On the night of January 21, 2012, Bychkov broke into a hardware store after hours, stealing three knives and 9,908 Russian rubles (about $315 at the time) from the till. Investigators found sufficient evidence to implicate Bychkov, and they arrested him several days later. Searching his home for any other stolen merchandise, they found instead a diary whose author called himself a "lone wolf," claimed credit for 11 murders, and blamed the woman who had spurned him for his crimes. Under interrogation, Bychkov added the grim twist of cannibalism, admitting that he had devoured hearts, livers, and muscle tissue excised from his victims. He directed police to six graves in his backyard at home, while evidence found in the house added two more murder counts, but proof remains elusive in the cases of his last two claimed victims.

In a classic understatement, one police spokesman told reporters that Bychkov had "formed a negative attitude towards the people who abused alcohol and led a beggary, roguish lifestyle." In preparation for his crimes, officers said, Bychkov had studied literature on other criminals and watched crime shows on television, and had "developed a criminal plan, prepared a weapon and studied the examples of similar crimes committed by serial killers." At the same time, he mastered "various strategies and methods to conceal crime traces, including the bodies of the victims."

Forensic psychiatrists diagnosed Bychkov as suffering from a "mixed personality disorder" — characterized by aggressive behavior disorder and chronic depression — but still found him legally sane and fit for trial. On March 22, 2013, the Penza Oblast Court convicted Alexander on nine counts of murder and one count of burglary, imposing a sentence of life imprisonment.

Psychiatrist Igor Yanushev seemed to question that verdict, telling the newspaper *Pravda* ("Truth"), "Such shocking crimes occur on a regular basis, even in much more socially advantaged countries than Russia. Foreign cannibals can be much more sophisticated in their perverted crimes than Russian ones. In Russia, believe me, cannibalism is much more prosaic, but its scale is more impressive. Every year, police catch several cannibals, and it goes about proved cases only. Usually, cannibals are mentally ill individuals. In most cases, cannibals get into medical, rather than penitentiary institutions after a verdict. A person, when recognized as mentally ill, undergoes compulsory medical treatment until he or she is healed. It doesn't last for life. After treatment, their case is reviewed again, and that's when they can face a criminal punishment. I personally know several cases when mental patients were recognized as healed and were released to freedom right from the courtroom. The statute of limitations expired. They can be released to freedom, despite the fact that they may commit their hideous crimes in 80 percent of cases."

Intrigued, journalists looked for more information and found it. During the very week of Bychkov's conviction, police in Vladivostok arrested an unnamed 35-year-old man who confessed to killing one of his friends and eating his body after a wild night of drinking. Officers found remnants of that meal in the offender's refrigerator. Earlier, in August 2010, Murmansk detectives had collared a 21-year-old man who confessed to killing and eating a victim he met on a gay dating website. Two months before that arrest, a court in the Perm region in the Ural Mountains imprisoned three homeless men who killed and ate a fourth, afterward selling the leftovers to a local kebab restaurant. And then, of course, in 2007, there had been the sensational case of "Chessboard Killer" Alexander Pichushkin (Chapter 13).

Bychkov's arrest set wheels turning toward Alexander Zhuplov's release from prison, but they moved slowly. Zhuplov's mother, Lyubov Zhuplova, filed a petition for her son's freedom with Russian Minister of Internal Affairs Rashid Nurgaliyev, but action on that plea was delayed until Bychkov had been convicted and sentenced in 2013, costing the innocent suspect another year of his life.

25. Artyom Anoufriev and Nikita Lytkin: "The Academy Maniacs"

A surprising number of serial killers operate with one or more accomplices in the commission of their crimes. Commonly dubbed "team killers," those predators feed each other's fantasies of murder, sexual assault, and any other crimes that obsess them, while the presence of a second offender — or several — may increase the odds of making mistakes that lead to capture and prison.

During 2010 and 2011, two sadistic friends staged a series of 15 attacks on residents of Akademgorodok ("Academic Town"), the educational and scientific center of Siberia, named for the presence within its borders of Novosibirsk State University, 35 research institutes, and a medical academy. Located 19 miles south of downtown Novosibirsk, Akademgorodok claims as its primary social center The House of Scientists, including a library with 100,000 volumes, a picture gallery, lecture venues and a concert hall.

All things considered, then, it's no surprise that Akademgorodok's team killers were nicknamed "The Academy Maniacs."

The older of the pair, Artyom Alexandrovich Anoufriev, was born on October 4, 1992, in Irkutsk, the administrative center of Irkutsk Oblast and one of Siberia's largest cities. His younger killing partner, Nikita Vakhtangovich Lytkin, was also born in Irkutsk, on March 24, 1993. Both were raised by single mothers, although Lytkin's father tried to reconcile the broken family on several occasions, always giving up and taking off again. Anoufriev's mother, Nina, an accountant for an insurance firm, was a misanthrope who publicly humiliated Artyom at any given opportunity, also warning him that he was constantly surrounded by enemies. Understandably depressed, he veered toward racism after an alleged attack by an Armenian gang that left him, in his mother's words, "psychologically damaged." Artyom countered that feeling by joining a "white power" skinhead gang and joining in the 2006 Russian March, a series of ultra-nationalist demonstrations aimed at countering Russia's Day of National Unity on November 4, wherein troops of thugs shouted at spectators, "This is our country!" When racists repeated their demonstration in November 2010, cameras caught Anoufriev wearing a gauze bandage labeled "Peoplehaters."

Nikita Lytkin's mother, Marina, worked as a shoe store clerk to support him, while her son's frustration and depression deepened toward his generally absent father. At trial, she would blame her ex-husband entirely for Nikita's antisocial behavior and slide into crime.

By the time Anoufriev met Lytkin at the birthday party of a mutual acquaintance, both were virtually friendless and withdrawn from civilized society, deeply depressed, and harboring morbid fantasies of random violence against strangers. Falling into chance conversation, they "clicked" immediately, each convinced that he had found a soul mate. As their twisted friendship grew, both readily agreed that the best solution for their rage would be a series of attacks on random strangers who, although unknown to them, they viewed as worthless dregs of the society they already despised. Both gained further inspiration by trolling the Internet for grisly facts about serial killers Alexander Pichushkin (Chapter 13) and Ukraine's "Dnepropetrovsk Maniacs," Viktor Sayenko and Igor Suprunyuck.

Over a span of five months, from November 2010 to April 2011, the Academy Maniacs prowled between the hours of 6:00 and 10:00 p.m., assaulting 16 victims by their own admission, each time using a knife and a mallet or baseball bat. Nine of those victims survived the attacks; six did not, and at least two murders were recorded for posterity on videotape.

Before attempting to kill anyone, the two friends decided to try practice runs. First, they bashed 18-year-old Anastasia Markov on the head with their mallet, then ran away laughing, leaving her bloodied but alive. Next, they ambushed a woman who remains unidentified, striking her in the same manner but that time stealing her purse.

Anoufriev and Lytkin claimed their first life, that of 12-year-old Danil Semyonov, on December 1, 2010, stunning the boy with a mallet, then fatally crushing his skull with a baseball bat. Incredibly, police in Akademgorodok filed Semyonov's murder away as an accidental death.

On December 16, the killers struck again, attacking 69-year-old Olga Pirog just 20 yards from the site of Danil Semyonov's slaying, stabbing her 30 times but leaving her valuables untouched. Because police had ruled the boy's death accidental, they saw no link between the incidents beyond a mere coincidence of geography. Artyom and Nikita also made a video recording of that crime, focused on

Pirog's mutilations and later released on social media, but it brought authorities no closer to the culprits.

On January 1, 2011, the killers claimed their third victim, a still-unidentified homeless man. They cracked his skull with a mallet and left him for passers-by to find, after which he died at a local hospital. Anonymous and with no known address, he was buried as "Corpse Number 20" when no one came forward to claim his remains.

Anoufriev and Lytkin took a seven-week hiatus after their second murder, then resurfaced on February 21. Victim Alexander Maximov had been out bar hopping until his cash ran low, at which point, drunk, he started off for home. Spotting him on the street, they staged another blitz attack, fracturing Maximov's skull and jaw. As he lay dying, they tried to excise one of his eyeballs, but their ignorance of human anatomy foiled the clumsy effort.

On March 11, the Academy Maniacs added an air gun to their arsenal, shooting homeless victim Roman Fayzullina twice in the head before they finished him off with a mallet and knife. Lytkin then tried to sever a hand, but his knife proved too small for the task, so he satisfied himself by cutting off Fayzullina's little finger.

The last murder victim—another homeless woman named Alevtina Kuydin—fell to the killers on April 3, 2011. Once again, they videotaped the slaying, but produced a record of failure as they tried to sever first an ear, then a hand, and finally an eyeball, all without success. Finally, they cut off one of Kuydin's earlobes and dropped it in front of a secondary school on their way home.

At that point, clumsy arrogance betrayed the Academy Maniacs. For taping murders, they had used a video camera owned by Nikita Lytkin's uncle — and after Kuydin's murder, Nikita foolishly left the camera's Secure Digital memory card in place. When Lytkin's uncle prepared to use the camera on April 5, he was shocked to behold a murder in progress. A rough transcript of that tape — all police cared to release for public consumption, follows:

Recording?
Yes.
A hobo! Ha-ha!
No one there? [Apparently referring to witnesses]
Fuck them!
[A knife pierces Kuydin's head.]
Fuck! I can't fucking touch it!
Don't touch anything!
[The blade saws at Kuydin's ear.]
Faster! There's nothing interesting.
But that's scary, eh, bitch?
[The knife penetrates Kuydin's eye.]
Uh, that's disgusting! What to do?
Cut off her hand. [Another failure]
Fuck it! An ear is fine, too.
Okay, let's go.

Aghast, Lytkin's uncle immediately called police, who arrested both killers the same afternoon. Investigation of the killing spree dragged on until March 2012, during which time forensic psychiatrists judged both defendants legally sane. An uproar of publicity produced conflicting portraits of the killers, some dubbing both neo-Nazis, while one article described Lytkin as a university medical student without providing further details. On April 2, 2013, a court in Irkutsk convicted both offenders. Artyom Anoufriev received a life prison term, while Nikita Lytkin — although only five months younger than his killing partner, at age 20 — was deemed "underage" and sentenced to 24 years in prison.

26. Still at Large: "The Granny Strangler"

We close *Iron Curtain Killers* with a troubling case which, at last published report, remains unsolved. This, despite the fact that police possess — and the global media has broadcast — multiple clear photographs of the only suspect, captured by closed circuit television cameras as he reconnoitered an apartment house occupied by prospective elderly victims. A sadistic gerontophile slayer, at last count he had claimed the lives of 32 women ranging in age from 75 to 90 years.

Most residents of the West know the Udmurt Republic — assuming they know it at all — as "the home of the Kalashnikov rifle," commonly known as the AK-47, widely considered by firearms enthusiasts and military personal as the finest, most efficient assault weapon ever invented. Even that is a mistake however, since the weapon's inventor, Lieutenant-General Mikhail Timofeyevich Kalashnikov of the Soviet Army (1919-2013) was actually born at Kurya, the administrative center of Altai Krai's Kuryinsky District. Kalashnikov did, however, *die* in Izhevsk, capital city of the Udmurt Republic, from a gastric hemorrhage at age 94. Nine years before his death, Izhevsk opened the M. T. Kalashnikov Museum and Small Arms Complex to honor his several inventions, drawing tourists from around the world.

Which brings us, by a backdoor, to our final tale. Udmurtia, like the rest of the former Soviet Union, has suffered from the dual plagues of alcohol and homicide since Communism's collapse in 1991. Writing for the journal *Social Science & Medicine* in

November 2002, authors V. V. Chervyakov, Vladimir M. Shkolnikov, Martin McKee, and William Alex Pridemore reported that Russia's murder rate was 20 times higher than that of Western Europe, and among the highest on Earth. Russia's standardized homicide rate increased by 81 percent between 1990 and 1999, with 81 percent of all convicted slayers claiming they were drunk at the time of their crimes. The authors also found that: "The nature of homicide in Russia has changed considerably in less than a decade, with many more now involving aggravating circumstances, such as murder to conceal another crime, in association with robbery or rape, or by a group of people...The characteristics of those convicted of homicide have also changed during the 1990s. They are now younger, less likely to have previous convictions, and to have a more diverse range of educational levels. The previous urban-rural gap, with higher levels in rural areas, has also narrowed."

Our present slayer's reign of terror began in 2011, and while he remained unidentified in published reports from February 2017, his acknowledged death toll stands at 32, murdered over the span of two years. Thus far, while the suspected killer's photos have blanketed print and electronic media, no list of his victims has been made available.

Police describe the killer as a sadist, emphasizing that he rarely steals money or any other items from his victims, but seems only drawn to strangle them inside their humble homes. From his behavior, infiltrating the flats of strangers, detectives suspect he may emulate the methods of imprisoned serial slayer Irina Gaidamachuk (Chapter 21) and may, in fact, be a "copycat killer." One indication of that possibility is found in testimony from surviving pensioners, who say a stranger appeared at their doors, claiming to represent their local government councils or the owners of their apartment blocks — tricks sometimes used by Gaidamachuk, who also misrepresented herself as a social worker. From that, detectives surmise that their unknown subject has not only studied Irina's case but may have access to official lists of elderly pension recipients.

In fact, police know much more about the killer today than when he began claiming victims in 2011. They now possess samples of his DNA, found on a handkerchief and a light, otherwise undescribed, left by their suspect at a crime scene in Yekaterinburg — Russia's fourth-largest city and the administrative center of Sverdlovsk Oblast — where he murdered two victims in 2012. Police files presently contain no matching samples from convicted criminals, but officers have even better evidence, consisting of multiple CCTV images that have captured the suspect while he scouted prospective victims.

The photos in question were recorded in October 2016, as the suspect moved about inside an apartment house with green-painted walls in Kazan, the capital and largest city of the Republic of Tatarstan, stalking hallways and entering an elevator. Police pegged his age somewhere between 25 and 35, his height at five feet six inches, with dark hair and eyes, a straight nose, "middle sized" lips, and a slender build. They also estimate his shoe size at 40 or 41, equivalent to a man's size 8 or 8½ in the United States. They further describe him as "an Asian national" of Tatar appearance, with Senior Investigator Ivan Streltsov adding, "We have serious grounds to suppose that he is a resident of Udmurtia" — where three victims were slain in the capital city. Furthermore, police believe their subject to be "a city rather than a rural man and to be of a low social and wealth level." His photos show him wearing a dark textile jacket, sports trousers, and athletic shoes.

Authorities released their CCTV photos of the suspect far and wide in February 2017 but, once again, without result. Confusion shrouds some aspects of the manhunt, as with the amount of the reward offered for information leading to the killer's capture, variously reported as ranging from 1 million to 3 million rubles ($17,400 to $52,200). Senior Investigator Streltsov broadcast the latter figure, adding, "If needed, we will guarantee anonymity." Streltsov also cautioned senior citizens that while the slayer had not claimed a victim in nearly five years, serial killers "can never stop themselves," and a fresh spate of murders in the making was suggested by the CCTV footage.

Part of the slayer's advantage over police is the far-ranging scope of his attacks during 2011 and 2012, roaming the vast western fringe of Siberia, including Chelyabinsk Oblast (33,900 square miles, with 3,476,217 inhabitants), Samara Oblast (20,700 square miles, 3,215,532 inhabitants), Sverdlovsk Oblast (75,200 square miles, population 4,297,747), the Republic of Tatarstan (26,000 square miles, population 3,786,488), and the Udmurt Republic (16,300 square miles, with 1,521,420 inhabitants).

In addition to the CCTV images, police have also reissued an Identi-Kit facial reconstruction of the suspect, composed with help from women he approached but left alive during 2011 and 2012, while warning all elderly shut-ins to exercise great caution before opening their doors to any strangers. Apparently, the killer has not struck again since publication of his candid photographs, nor has he been identified. The state reward — whatever its amount, in fact — remains unclaimed.

And in the meantime, the authorities, along with his prospective victims, wait in fear.

About the Author

Michael Newton has published 318 books since becoming a freelance professional author in 1977. His previous work for RJ Parker Publications includes two standalone true-crime biographies, *The Dark Strangler* (2015) and *Hangman* (2016), plus 10 biographical chapters on various slayers in Parker's groundbreaking annual *Serial Killer True Crime Anthologies* (2014-2017).

Published under his own name and various pseudonyms, Newton is known for his *Encyclopedia of Serial Killers* (1st ed. 2000, 2nd ed. 2005), a bestseller for Facts on File. His history of the Florida Ku Klux Klan, *The Invisible Empire,* won the Florida Historical Society's Rembert Patrick Award as "Best Book in Florida History" for 2002. In 2006, the American Library Association honored his *Encyclopedia of Cryptozoology* as one of the year's twelve Outstanding Reference Works. Writing as "*Lyle Brandt*," Newton won the Western Fictioneers' first Peacemaker Award for Best Western Novel of 2010 for *Manhunt.* Another "Brandt" novel, *Avenging Angels,* was also a Peacemaker Best Novel finalist in 2011, as well as being a Best Paperback Original finalist for the Western Writers of America's Spur Award in 2011. His novel *West of the Big River: The Avenging Angel* was nominated as a Peacemaker Best Novel in 2014. Newton lives with his wife Heather in Indiana. Readers may contact him by email through his website at *www.michaelnewton.homestead.com*, and follow him on his Facebook page at https://www.facebook.com/MichaelNewtonAuthor.

Amazon Author Page

34152590R00079

Made in the USA
Lexington, KY
19 March 2019